THE HEART
REVOLUTION

THE HEART REVOLUTION

EXPERIENCE THE POWER OF A TURNED HEART

Sergio De La Mora

BakerBooks

a division of Baker Publishing Group
Grand Rapids, Michigan

Published by Baker Books
a division of Baker Publishing Group
P.O. Box 6287, Grand Rapids, MI 49516-6287

Printed in the United States of America

ISBN 978-0-8010-1384-3

This book is dedicated to my father, Salvador De La Mora, who has been my greatest hero and source of vision and inspiration. In our society, few men have had the privilege to be fathered, and even fewer men have had a father who they can love, respect, and honor. Words will never be able to express the sense of pride I have for my father. Everything that I am is because of him. I am so grateful to God that I am the son of Salvador De La Mora. I love you, Dad!

Quiero dedicar este libro a mi padre, Salvador De La Mora, quien ha sido mi héroe más grande y la fuente de visión e inspiración. En nuestra sociedad, pocos hombres han tenido el privilegio de experimentar el verdadero amor paternal, y aun menos han tenido un padre a quien ellos puedan amar, respetar y honrar. Las palabras nunca podrán expresar el sentimiento de orgullo que le tengo a mi padre. Todo lo que soy se lo debo a Él. Estoy tan agradecido con Dios de ser el hijo de Salvador De La Mora. Te amo, Papa!

Contents

Contents

Foreword

Every one of us—no matter what profession we practice, what culture we live in, or what economic demographic we are a part of—would admit that there is something about our lives that we would like to change. From housewives to truck drivers to CEOs, we all would confess there is some aspect, some dimension of our existence we would like to tweak, shift, or alter. Yet, while we may seek change today, so often the catalyst for our desire has very little to do with our present circumstances and has everything to do with our past experiences.

Maybe you can point back to a time in your life when you were hurt by someone. And now, the memory of it is keeping you tethered to the past. Or perhaps you remember a time when you were the one who hurt someone else. And the guilt, shame, and embarrassment you feel are the very things holding you back.

Whether we are the ones who are hurting or the ones who have hurt, the pain we feel is real. It goes beyond our mind and reaches deep into our soul. And while we may not fully understand it, we know we want to change it. We want to

13

move from experiencing the pain to taking hold of a new purpose.

But how? Where do we turn? What can we do to begin experiencing the change we so desperately want?

Those are all relevant questions that, when answered, will help lead to true, lasting change. And when we are determined to not only ask the questions but then actively seek the answers, we discover a powerful reality: while change often brings with it conflict, on the other side we find phenomenal growth! That is the spin cycle of success: *change—conflict—growth*. And it all starts in one place—the heart.

From the outset of this book, my good friend Sergio De La Mora reveals to us that all this needed change is first and foremost a heart issue. And he shows us the only way to experience true change is by turning to God and opening our hearts to Him.

As Sergio says, "Only in the depths of a person's heart can God bring healing, purpose, and hope for a new beginning."

This book is a work of devotion, born out of Sergio's desire to help all people discover all that God has in store for their lives—beyond the pain. His passion and heart for people is evident in every word and through every sentence. And as you read these pages, you will discover that the cycle toward lasting change begins when you open your heart, turn it toward God, and ask Him to begin your *Heart Revolution*.

Ed Young Jr.
senior pastor, Fellowship Church
author, *Outrageous, Contagious Joy*

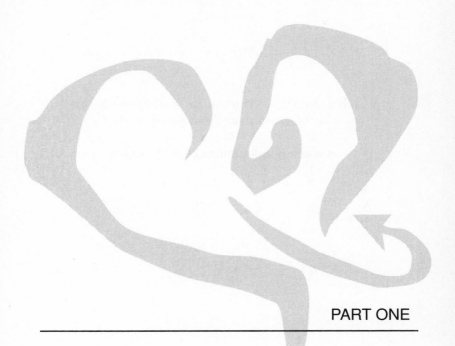

PART ONE

YOU AND THE REVOLUTION

Watch a special video message from Pastor Sergio
Part One: You and the Revolution

www.sergiodelamora.com/heartrev

1

Captured by the Revolution

Every generation needs a new revolution.

—Thomas Jefferson

This book is all about your heart.

Our society has underestimated the value of the heart. We spend millions of dollars educating people's minds and overlook the importance of educating a person's heart. While I believe in educating and empowering the minds of the next generation, it is equally important to educate and empower their hearts.

When God was looking to choose a king to lead His people, His primary prerequisite was not the intellectual level of the potential king but the quality of his heart (1 Sam. 16:7). Your heart is your most valuable asset. It's the epicenter of your life, and out of it comes your deepest pains, your greatest

17

triumphs. Your journey for the next forty days begins and ends at the center of your life—your heart.

The stories, the trials, and the triumphs you are about to read are genuine testimonies to the life-changing power of God that continues to manifest itself every day.

Use your pain to produce a new power that will propel you to live an unimaginable life!

You and I have been called to become revolutionaries. You have been called to overthrow systems of belief that cannot produce for you the life you truly desire to live. Most people feel powerless because of their pain, but now is the time to begin to use your pain to produce a new power that will propel you to live an unimaginable life—a life marked by a new beginning with a new perspective and a new passion to pursue, overtake, and recover all that belongs to you!

During times of struggle and disappointment, our vision often becomes blurred. We lose the ability to clearly see our present circumstances and future promises. It's during these moments, when we feel powerless to move forward in our lives, that God shows up to silence the daunting voice of the unknown.

I had such a moment. This book, *The Heart Revolution*, began with my own heart revolution, and if God can turn my heart, He can turn anyone's heart.

I was raised in Santa Barbara, California, the youngest of six children. My parents were immigrants from Mexico, and though they were able to find success here in America, we struggled to belong. My brothers and their friends started a gang that I inevitably joined in order to avoid getting beat up every day after school. I quickly got caught up in the life of gangs and drugs and began smoking PCP by the age of thirteen.

In eighth grade my life took a turn. That was the year I was stabbed in my back and almost paralyzed. My parents forced me to stay home, and I got hooked on a college radio station, KCSB. I didn't know it then, but destiny had intervened in my life. Every weekend I would listen to this DJ, captivated by his ability to move me by his words. I discovered this local college radio station had a special program for DJs, regardless of age, who wanted to get their Federal Communications Commission (FCC) license. So here I was a fifteen-year-old *cholo*, or gang member, who went down to the UCSB campus and got my license to become a disc jockey. Though I didn't know it at the time, that one decision saved me from a gang life.

I went on to start a DJ company, which ended up growing to be the largest in Santa Barbara's history. I was sixteen years old, on the radio promoting anything and everything. I was doing party after party throughout the city, and I loved it. I was making more money than a teenager should ever be allowed to make, and I was on the verge of signing a seven-year record contract as a disc jockey. If you had asked anyone around me how I was doing, they would have told you I was successful, happy, and together. I wasn't. I was hooked on cocaine and locked in a life I ultimately didn't want. Deep down I knew it was only a matter of time before everything I worked for would come crashing down. But rather than confront my issues, I chose to lose myself to an addiction that threatened to end my life.

It's hard to believe that one moment can change a person's life, but that's exactly what happened to me. On August 4, 1984, I was passing out flyers during Fiestas, promoting one of my notorious dances on State Street, when I picked up a different flyer promoting a church called Cornerstone Church of Santa Barbara—a church I would later come to love. The flyer read, "Jesus Christ is coming back. Are you ready?"

The instant I picked it up, I remembered a dream I had a week prior as I was considering this record contract. In my dream, I was standing in front of a fork in a dirt road. A sign showed two directions: "worldly success" and "ministry."

God seemed to be saying to me, "If you sign that contract, you'll have success, but you'll miss the purpose for your life. Sergio, follow Me."

I remember thinking, "Ministry?" I hadn't even been interested in following God, let alone devoting my life to serve Him. I brushed it off, but kept the flyer.

Out of desperation for something different in my life, I attended the advertised event a few days later. I was a jumble of emotions—hopeful but terrified, expectant but ashamed. Sitting in the back row, I thought about the irony of that church being the same place I had held dances at in the past. But tonight was different. I wasn't there for a party. I was there because I wanted to end the party. I needed my heart turned. I was tired of the constant battle between who I was and who I needed to be. Trapped in the drug culture of the entertainment industry, I knew I couldn't get out on my own. So the night before I had come to church, I had done two things. One, I did half a gram of cocaine, because I never went anywhere without being high. And two, I told God these words: "If You can change my life and take this monkey off my back, I'll do whatever You want."

As the pastor talked about Christ's death on the cross opening the door for us to experience God's love and forgiveness, I felt like I was the only person in the room. Could it be true? Could God really love me? I was high, I was an ex-gang member from the 'hood, and I had turned my back on God. Didn't that make me unacceptable?

No, the pastor assured us, God's forgiveness covers every sin, and His love brings light to even the darkest heart. For the past few years, people had tried to tell me about Christ, but I had dismissed them. That day, though, things were different.

At the end of his message, the pastor asked, "Does anyone want to receive Christ?" I raised my hand. Then he said, "If you do, come forward." With my hand still raised and tears streaming down my face, I stepped out into the aisle and walked to the front of the room.

At that moment I knew that my life was about to change radically. I simply couldn't say yes to Jesus and go back to the life I'd been living. I remember telling myself, "I'm going to do whatever it takes to walk out this new life. I may fall, but I'll get back up. I won't stop pursuing God. People may laugh at me and misunderstand me, but I will refuse to live from their opinion of me!"

That night I went to work at the KMYX radio station as usual, but even then, I knew the revolution had already begun in my heart. When I sat down in front of the microphone, I began to introduce a very popular song, just as I had countless times before. But this time, I said, "And now here is an artist who is talking about the 666!" I sat back in a daze, unsure of what had just happened, and realized I wasn't the same person anymore. My heart had turned and my life had changed. I was now captured by the revolution! My station manager called me on the phone and growled, "What was that?!" When I said nothing, he yelled, "We'll talk tomorrow!"

> **I couldn't say yes to Jesus and go back to the life I'd been living.**

The next day I shared with him about my new commitment to Christ. He replied with a smile, "Sergio, you're just going through a phase. Lots of people do. You'll be fine. Don't make any rash decisions. What you really want is more money." He offered me a bigger take on the income from commercials, and he said he'd have Wolfman Jack tape the intro to my show. But I told him, "No, that's no longer who I am. I'm leaving the station."

In the weeks to come, I sold my DJ company, left the show, sold my state-of-the-art sound system, and stopped promoting dances. Suddenly, in the eyes of my fans, I went from a hero to a zero. I had lost everything, but in losing it I had found far more. Immediately I got committed to my local church and started serving in any area they needed. Instead of using my van to transport my sound equipment to dances,

I transported equipment and people to church. I cleaned the restrooms, set up chairs, and served as their soundman.

God is telling you, "Dream anyway, believe anyway!"

As I continued to walk out my new commitment to Christ, God opened new doors for me as disc jockey on a Christian radio station in Carpinteria, California. My heart was so full of God's love, captured by this revolution, that I took every opportunity to tell young people about Jesus.

A revolution of the heart, like I experienced, only occurs when we are willing to look inside and take bold steps to overthrow the old mindsets and habits that live dormant in our hearts. If we're not careful, the voice of our past will cause us to slip back into those familiar patterns. Choose today to be different by refusing to allow the pain of your past to hold you back from a new level of living!

God never designed us to live with small dreams and purposes. Our old life tells us, "Don't live with expectancy. Don't let your hopes get too high because you might get disappointed." But God is telling you, "Dream anyway, believe anyway!"

Sometimes the people closest to you, who know your pain, can be the very ones who confine you because they're afraid for you. They don't want to see you experience any more hurt than you've already had. So with good intentions, they ask you to downsize your dreams to fit the disappointing demands of your circumstances. But with a revolutionized heart, you can break free from your hurt, your pain, and your fear. Paul assures us that Christ's love for us and in us gives us more than enough power to conquer anything:

> Yet in all these things we are more than conquerors through Him who loved us. (Rom. 8:37)

When I decided to allow God to revolutionize my heart, I didn't know that so many lives would be affected by that one decision. I didn't know I would be writing this book. I didn't know Georgina and I, along with our children, would have the privilege of founding Cornerstone Church of San Diego, one of the fastest growing churches in America. I didn't know God would use the seven families who came with us from Santa Barbara to raise a generation of leaders wholeheartedly committed to turning hearts back to God and back to their family. And I didn't know that God would use our church to start a nationwide Heart Revolution. All I knew back then was that I needed God to turn my life around and end the pain I was going through.

Instead of seeing a teenager trapped in a life of gangs and drugs, God saw a pastor hidden in that young seventeen-year-old.

What does He see hidden inside of you?

The purpose of this book is to encourage you to take this 40-Day Heart Challenge and discover who God sees inside you! Allow this book to be your guide through the next forty days, as you learn to live, love, and lead from your heart. I challenge you to read a chapter a day and give God the opportunity to revolutionize your life. For an inspiring Heart Revolution message from Sergio De La Mora, visit us online at

www.sergiodelamora.com/heartrev

The change you've been looking for is locked within the pages of this book. Open your heart, and as you do that, get ready for God to launch you into your destiny.

Let the *Heart Revolution* begin.

2

Finding Purpose in Pain

Healing is not the resolution of our past; it is the
use of our past to draw us into deeper relationship
with God and his purpose for our lives.

—Dan Allender, psychologist

Remember *The Wizard of Oz*'s Tin Man who didn't
have a heart? How many people have thought at one
time or another that life would be much easier if they
had been born without a heart—a life seemingly without
hurt, regret, or heartache?

As I have matured and walked closer with God, I have
discovered our heart is the very power source of our life.
The heart is where God's greatest deposits are made, the
level where He often teaches us life's most important lessons.
Only in the depths of a person's heart can God bring healing,

purpose, and hope for a new beginning. And when healing is experienced at a heart level, the result is true freedom.

In the book of Romans, the apostle Paul depicts the freedom God offers through His Son—freedom from the most painful of experiences.

> So now there is no condemnation for those who belong to Christ Jesus. And because you belong to him, the power of the life-giving Spirit has freed you from the power of sin that leads to death. (Rom. 8:1–2 NLT)

Your past doesn't have to punish your future! Even more powerful is God's declaration to us that He is personally involved with our hurts and has a plan for every situation:

> My grace is sufficient for you, for My strength is made perfect in weakness. (2 Cor. 12:9)

How encouraging it is to know that, regardless of your situation, your pain is not in vain.

Say it again to yourself: *My pain is not in vain!*

Today you may be discouraged because you've placed your heart in the wrong hands, but God wants you to know with confidence that He is willing and able to heal the broken places of your heart and restore your hope for tomorrow.

When we allow God to see all the pieces, we give Him permission to turn any hurt we place in His hands into our greatest strength. Oftentimes the pain we've been running from is exactly what God wants us to run toward. Viewing painful situations in this way is a revolutionary concept for a society that tends to avoid and numb pain. But I firmly believe God is saying to you today, "Give your heart to Me and I'll use the very situation you're going through to bring the best out of you. I can use it to set you up to succeed!"

While times of difficulty may not feel good at the moment, they are often God's scalpel to perform heart surgery in order for Him to bring healing and restoration to the condition of our hearts. Your breakthrough is right on the other side of that situation. Believe this: God can break you through!

Years of counseling others have shown me that many people do not know what to do with the pain they've experienced. No one has taught them to pay attention to what God is saying to them through their struggles, so they're forced to face their pain with confusion and doubt. They are tempted to play the blame game or hide behind the shroud of denial.

God can turn any hurt we place in His hands into our greatest strength.

Let's face it, it's easier to blame others than to take responsibility for our own decisions and to take the hard steps necessary to make things right. But one step today in the right direction can put you back on the right path. Right now, you can make the decision to turn your heart back to God and back to your family and begin to revolutionize the areas of your life you may have been trying to forget. God releases to each of us the power to stop marginalizing our pain and instead to begin leveraging it to make significant gains. The very thing that threatened to crush your heart can be the tool God uses to launch you into your God-given destiny!

Oftentimes we struggle with the idea of a God-given destiny because we have been beaten down by pain, either inherited or self-inflicted. When a person has wrestled with inherited pain, they often lose their fight to win, because circumstances out of their control have broken their heart. A parent or a spouse walked out, beat them, or verbally broke their spirit with sarcasm and criticism. They had no control over—so they weren't responsible for—a family member or loved one who was an addict or a liar or MIA. The victim mentality rears its head, threatening to steal their joy and hope for greater things.

Self-inflicted pain, on the other hand, is the product of our own choices. We're haunted by decisions we wish we'd never made. Whether they were planned or snap decisions, they have hurt us.

In God's eyes it doesn't make any difference whether our pain is inherited or self-inflicted. In every moment and in every kind of hurt, God is willing and able to convert it into our greatest strength. He longs for us to turn to Him so that we can understand His plans and purposes for our life. No matter the pain, no matter the circumstance, God wants you to know He can turn it around, just as the psalmist's words describe:

> You changed my sorrow into dancing.
>   You took away my clothes of sadness,
>   and clothed me in happiness. (Ps. 30:11 NCV)

Scientists have figured out how to tap into the benefits of recycling by converting hydrogen into fuel for cars. The result is power and a little water, both very good things. On a much bigger scale, green plants all over the planet use photosynthesis to change carbon dioxide, which is poisonous at high levels, into life-giving oxygen. In the same way, God has the amazing capacity to convert even the most poisonous things in our lives into life, strength, and insight—if we trust Him. Even in our darkest moments, God is a source of light. We may not have the full picture until we see Him face-to-face, but we can be confident that He knows, He cares, and He is working everything together for good. That's what Paul meant when he wrote to the Christians in Rome,

> We know that all things work together for good to those who love God, to those who are the called according to His purpose. (Rom. 8:28)

Reaching beyond the pulpit and connecting with people on a deeper, more personal level remains one of my greatest joys as a pastor. A few years ago, I was making calls to connect with people who had come to our church for the first time. I wanted to personally thank them for coming to visit us. That morning I had several very pleasant conversations, and then I made a call I will never forget. On the other end was Chris,* a man who was, to say the least, resistant to my call. I asked if he had enjoyed coming to our church, and he responded, "Not really." Sensing God's hand on this man's life, I asked him to consider coming back and giving us another shot, but he replied, "Why should I? What's the use?"

From my evangelism training, I knew that a cynical response is often a sign of a broken heart. I challenged him. "If you'll give God and our church another chance, you won't regret it."

The word "regret" caused an explosion in Chris's heart. This man had lived for years with gnawing regrets. He confided in me that he had done some unspeakable things. "God knows everything you've done," I said, "and He loves you, Chris. You don't have to be perfect, just willing to be perfected." He was stunned that I was still talking with him, after all he'd confessed to me, and soon his heart softened. As our conversation continued, he began to trust me enough to open his heart and share more of his life's story. I didn't try to mend all of Chris's wounds during that conversation; just listening was enough medicine at that point. I had no idea whether I would ever talk to him again.

The next Sunday after the service, a man walked up to me and introduced himself. It was Chris! I remember giving him a hug and telling him how much I loved and appreciated him for giving God and the church another chance. Over the next few months, God did an amazing transformation in his life. He became convinced that God's love and forgiveness could reach even into the shattered remains of his heart and make it new. As we met together over the following weeks, Chris opened his heart even more and told me more about the areas

* To protect the privacy of the individuals whose stories have been shared by the author, most names have been changed.

of his life that desperately needed the transforming power of God—the details of abuse he had endured, the rejection and condemnation he had felt growing up surrounded by religion, his cocaine habit that temporarily numbed the pain when he left home, the string of broken relationships that littered his past, the shame he had of abandoning his daughter, and the desperation that ultimately led to several suicide attempts.

At every point of transparency, God met him and began healing his deep hurts. Chris began the incredible journey of seeing God restore hope, renew his purpose for living, and give him a bigger, more loving family than he ever imagined. Years later, I had the privilege of introducing him to the woman who eventually became his lovely wife and the mother of his children. Today Chris's family has joined the Heart Revolution and is now ministering to over a thousand families in our church every week.

Come on, somebody! That's the power of a turned heart!

For many years, pain had caused Chris to isolate himself from God, from his family, from his daughter, and from other people, but during a simple conversation on the phone that day, God began the miracle of reconciliation in his heart. The shame he had experienced for so long finally revealed his desperate need for God, and God used the pain he had endured to show him how much He loved him. "If God can love and forgive me," he told me months later, "He can love and forgive anybody."

Respond to God's call in your life and allow Him to revolutionize your heart. He's closer than you think, He's more ready to forgive than you can imagine, and He longs to love you more than you can comprehend!

3

Our Deepest Pains,
Our Greatest Lessons

God whispers to us in our success, but shouts in
our pain.

—C. S. Lewis

As a father, I remember several occasions when my wife, Georgina, and I had to step back and allow our girls to learn some lessons the hard way. No matter how difficult, we knew it was in these key moments that we as parents were giving our children tools that would eventually shape their character and moral philosophies. We had to see beyond the present and resist the temptation to rush in and "fix it" for them. As a result of these formative seasons, we've seen our kids learn to choose consistently to *grow* through situations rather than simply *go* through them.

In my own life and in the lives of countless others, God models this same principle to teach two important lessons: respect and honor. I will never forget one example of this in my own life. It was when my father had to teach me how to respect and honor my relationship with God over my personal agenda. I was eleven years old and skateboarding was my world. At every moment of every day, I was looking for the next time I could grab my board and hit the streets. I was on my way to becoming a semi-professional skateboarder, and every day of practice was important.

Choose to *grow* through situations rather than simply *go* through them.

Now, being a De La Mora means certain things: you never come to the dinner table without something to say about your day, you always know Saturdays are landscaping days with Dad—and Sundays are church days. Period. My parents' rule on Sundays was, we were free to do whatever we wanted, but only until 4:00 p.m. Sunday mass was at 4:30 p.m. and every one of us was expected to be home and ready to go together as a family. It was our Sunday ritual, and nothing—and I do mean nothing—got in its way.

Well, one Sunday I was out skateboarding at The Bowl in beautiful Montecito, California. That day I was determined to learn how to drop into The Bowl without crashing and burning. I glanced at my watch. 3:50 p.m. I decided I wasn't ready to leave. I was *hot* that day—everything was working right. I just needed more time. My dad would understand—this was my future. I looked at my watch. 3:56 p.m. I jumped on my board and dropped in. I stayed out on The Bowl, hitting my drop-ins harder and harder each time, convincing myself it was time well spent. I was confident I had made the right decision. As the sun began to set, I peeked at my watch again. 5:15 p.m. Time to go home.

I crept through the kitchen door, pausing to listen for the voices of my brothers and sisters. I was greeted only by a sickening silence. My confidence came crashing down as the minutes ticked by while I waited for my family to come home. 6:43 p.m. The car doors slammed and the waves of voices came through the kitchen door. My oldest brother walked in first, glanced at me, and smirked, shaking his head as he carried a bag of groceries to the table. Immediately I went into survival mode—fake it to make it. Feigning confidence, I stepped toward the door, as though nothing was wrong, to help unload the rest of the groceries with everyone else. The muffled laughter and quiet badgering of my siblings began to get louder. But my parents said nothing. That is, until every bag of food had been put away. Then the inevitable happened.

My dad looked at me with eyes of disappointment that took my breath away. I had no idea what was about to happen. "Go get your skateboard and meet me outside," he said.

Incredulous, I thought, *Maybe he wants me to show him my tricks! Maybe I'm not in trouble after all!* I grabbed my board and ran outside, ready to show off my skills. He looked at me and said, "Give it to me, Sergio." Fear raced down my back as I placed my most prized possession into his outstretched hand. He slammed it against the curb with more force than I'd ever seen him use. I stared at my skateboard, still intact in his hand, and stammered in teenage arrogance, "Dad, that's oak wood. It won't break."

He said, "It may not break, Sergio, but it will burn." My dad turned, walked into the house, and threw my beloved board into the fireplace. Then he lit a match and set it aflame. I watched through tears as my skateboard burned before my eyes. My brothers and sisters stood speechless behind me. It was the greatest pain I had ever known.

I can still hear my father's next words: "Sergio, nothing in your life will ever come before God again. Put Him first and you can have anything. Put Him second and you'll have nothing."

That day was the moment everything changed in my relationship with God. My father taught me a lesson that still burns in my heart today. Believe it or not, that experience produced a greater respect and honor for God than ever before. And my father's words gave me a larger vision and direction for my future. If you will allow God to revolutionize your most painful situations, He will reveal that you are at the brink of your turning point!

Without God's perspective, we miss out on some of His greatest lessons found in this tension between joy and tribulation. Think of a car battery. It fulfills its purpose through its power that comes from both a positive and a negative current running through it. When a car battery runs out of power, we give it a jump-start by hooking up both positive and negative cables. The tension of joy and tribulation in our lives works the same way. We need *both* positive and negative currents to energize our purpose and call. Painful situations "ground" us in ways that joyful situations cannot. But the good news is, when we turn our hearts to Jesus Christ, who has ultimately triumphed over tribulations, we can experience what He promises in His Word:

Painful situations "ground" us in ways that joyful situations cannot.

> I have told you these things, so that in Me you may have [perfect] peace and confidence. In the world you have tribulation and trials and distress and frustration; but be of good cheer [take courage; be confident, certain, undaunted]! For I have overcome the world. [I have deprived it of power to harm you and have conquered it for you.] (John 16:33 AMP)

God's goal for our lives isn't to simply make us happy. His desire is to make us holy—more like Him. When I talk to people who are hurting, I remind them that Jesus knew shame, ridicule, and rejection. He endured incredible pain, and through it, the writer to the Hebrews tells us a mystery: the perfect Son of God "learned obedience from what he suffered" (5:8 NIV). He learned to depend on the Father more than ever. If we'll pay attention, we'll see God is using every situation to give us the opportunity to depend on Him more than we ever have before!

Author and professor J. I. Packer observed that God has a greater purpose than helping us avoid pain:

> This is what all the work of grace aims at—an even deeper knowledge of God, and an ever closer fellowship with Him. Grace is God drawing us sinners closer and closer to Him. How does God in grace prosecute this purpose? Not by shielding us from assault by the world, the flesh, and the devil, nor by protecting us from burdensome and frustrating circumstances, nor yet by shielding us from troubles created by our own temperament and psychology; but rather by exposing us to all these things, so as to overwhelm us with a sense of our own inadequacy, and to drive us to cling to Him more closely. This is the ultimate reason, from our standpoint, why God fills our lives with troubles and perplexities of one sort or another—it is to ensure that we shall learn to hold Him fast.[1]

How do you and I respond when we feel "overwhelmed with a sense of our own inadequacy"? We may be tempted to hide, fight back, or blame others, but if we do these things, we miss God's still small voice beckoning us to come closer to Him. And as we draw close to Him, we find the confidence that He is greater than our present circumstance.

One of the privileges I enjoy as a pastor is watching people discover their God-given potential as they open up their hearts and live more abundantly than they ever imagined. The apostle Paul gives the same challenge to the church in Corinth:

> Dear, dear Corinthians, I can't tell you how much I long for you to enter this wide-open, spacious life. We didn't fence you in. The smallness you feel comes from within you. Your lives aren't

small, but you're living them in a small way. . . . Open up your lives. Live openly and expansively! (2 Cor. 6:11–13 Message)

Opening your heart doesn't come without the risk of being hurt. But never allow yourself to think that God will waste a hurt. Hurt is a precious commodity to Him, which He transfers to your account so that you can learn invaluable lessons.

Some of the greatest lessons I've seen unfold from pain have been in the life of a good friend of mine who has journeyed with me for many years. The pain Eric carried was rooted in the brutal reality that, for the entirety of his life, his father refused to acknowledge Eric as his son, even to the point that invitations to family events would never come. For years, weddings, birthdays, and funerals were just reminders that, in his father's eyes, Eric did not exist. It was his deepest pain.

Hurt is a precious commodity to God.

As Eric grew up, he made decisions based on this pain. Everything that came into Eric's life was filtered through one emotion: anger. It was his coping mechanism and his security. Though he couldn't change his father's rejection, he could prevent anyone else from getting close enough to add salt to his wounds.

One day God got ahold of his life through a woman who saw past his anger. Her love for him brought him to a church service that changed his life. Eric found himself on his knees in front of a Father who would never abandon him and never reject him. Over the years I have seen God transform his heart and the pain of his father's rejection. Eric discovered the courage to get better instead of bitter as he used the pain and rejection of his father to draw him closer to God. As a result, God gave him the opportunity to minister to others in ways he never could have imagined. Today he is a primary leader of large groups of our men and women. Through his deepest pain, he learned some of life's most valuable lessons. He now transfers this knowledge to those he leads—lessons such as:

- Being rejected by someone doesn't mean you'll be rejected by everyone.
- Never give up on someone, even when they've given up on you.
- Until it costs you to love someone, you haven't really loved them.
- Just because something happened to you doesn't mean you have to repeat it.

Eric couldn't avoid struggle and heartache, but he learned how to stop the generational curse of rejection from continuing in the relationship between him and his son. He started believing that God was able to do exceedingly abundantly above all that he could ask, think, or imagine, and that is exactly what God has done!

"Ambidextrous faith" trusts God in the good times and the bad.

In his book *Reaching for the Invisible God*, Philip Yancey recounts, "Gregory of Nyssa once called St. Basil's faith 'ambidextrous' because he welcomed pleasures with the right hand and afflictions with the left, convinced both would serve God's design for him."[2] When we are convinced that God has good purposes for our pain, we gain "ambidextrous faith," trusting Him in the good times and the bad to teach us life's most valuable lessons.

Remember—**what you see when your eyes are closed is more important than what you see when they are open.** Close your eyes and make the decision to see your greatest pains as your greatest lessons!

4

The Pain to Become

Everyone struggles to become the person they have
been called to be. Even a caterpillar will struggle
to become a butterfly before it can spread its wings
and fly.

—Anonymous

My family owns a landscape company that my parents,
Salvador and Soledad De La Mora, started years
ago. Even at the age of nine, I worked in the family
business. I raked leaves and did whatever else my dad needed
me to do—but I didn't like it. Most kids on Friday were really
excited about the weekend, but not me. The weekend meant
waking up at 7:00 a.m. and going to work with my dad. At
school, while other kids asked each other about their spring
break or summer vacation plans, no one asked me because
they already knew. I was going landscaping with my dad. It
wasn't that my father was trying to deprive me of vacations.

It was because my father believed in discipline. He believed in me. He knew that, unless I became personally acquainted with the pain of discipline, I could never become who God was calling me to be. My dad knew there was a winner inside of me, but I needed discipline to get it out! He would always tell me, "The disciplined man always wins." My dad must have understood the biblical insight found in the book of Hebrews:

> No discipline seems pleasant at the time, but painful. Later on, however, it produces a harvest of righteousness and peace for those who have been trained by it. (Heb. 12:11 NIV)

One Saturday morning as we got out of his truck, I complained, "Dad, it's really hard to come to work, especially on Saturday morning. Can't I go home?"

He looked at me and gave me one of the most profound answers I've ever heard. He said, "Son, life is 20 percent joy, and 80 percent pain. If you will embrace the 80 percent of pain in your life and learn from it, you'll be able to really enjoy the 20 percent of pleasure, without regrets." I stood there soaking in all he was saying, but he wasn't finished. "If you'll commit yourself to take responsibility, show up on time, do a good job even when you'd rather be doing something else, you'll have something that no one can ever take away from you: character."

My dad, Salvador De La Mora, is the wisest, most humble, and most godly man I've ever known. His words that day burned into my heart like a branding iron. People often struggle to become who they've been called to be because they've never had a father who modeled to them what my father modeled to me. Perhaps you weren't raised with this kind of father. I want you to believe with me, regardless of who was or was not there in your life, God is ready now to father you through your struggle to *become*! To become the husband or wife, the father or mother, the leader, the *person* God knows you can be.

Facing the test to become requires tremendous courage because it means dealing with the baggage in your life. Every one of us comes to a point in our lives where, in order to move forward, we must let go of our past.

One of the most tragic stories in the Bible is the story of King

In order to move forward, we must let go of our past.

Saul. By all outward appearances, he was everything a leader should be—handsome, tall, strong, and wealthy—but when it came time for him to become king, Saul found himself at a familiar location—hiding behind the baggage of insecurity, fear, and doubt.

> So Samuel brought all the tribes of Israel before the LORD. . . . But when they looked for [Saul], he had disappeared! So they asked the LORD, "Where is he?"
> And the LORD replied, "He is hiding among the baggage." (1 Sam. 10:20–22 NLT)

What I love about God is that He did not disqualify Saul from becoming king because he was hiding among his baggage. As with Saul, becoming who God has called you to be is going to require you to come out from behind your baggage. Baggage—whether it is spiritual, emotional, relational, or even physical—will always seem more comfortable, more familiar, and somehow safer than stretching to become who you are called to be. But God will call you from where you are to where you're going because He sees the greatness of your future! Believe God as He declares to you that you can overcome the pain of your past to become the man or woman He has already predestined you to be! You can outlive the person you may have been, because God has promised—in fact, it's His solemn vow—to transform you from the inside by helping you rise up from life's most difficult and painful problems and disappointments.

> And I will give you a new heart, and I will put a new spirit in you. I will take out your stony, stubborn heart and give you

a tender, responsive heart. And I will put my Spirit in you so that you will follow my decrees and be careful to obey my regulations. (Ezek. 36:26–27 NLT)

Perhaps the baggage holding you back is the fear of failure. Perhaps you feel like you've made too many mistakes or made too many wrong decisions, and now you find yourself afraid to try again. Or maybe the baggage you're hiding behind is the opposite—the fear of success. Maybe the fear of constantly having to live under the high expectations from previous successes has left you living a marginal life.

Read this incredible quote penned by author Marianne Williamson and let its message strengthen your heart:

> Our deepest fear is not that we are inadequate. Our deepest fear is that we are powerful beyond measure. It is our light, not our darkness that most frightens us. We ask ourselves, Who am I to be brilliant, gorgeous, talented, fabulous? Actually, who are you *not* to be? You are a child of God. Your playing small does not serve the world. There is nothing enlightened about shrinking so that other people won't feel insecure around you. We are all meant to shine, as children do. We were born to make manifest the glory of God that is within us. It's not just in some of us; it's in everyone. And as we let our own light shine, we unconsciously give other people permission to do the same. As we are liberated from our own fear, our presence automatically liberates others.[3]

God is calling you today to take the first step and begin to let go of whatever baggage is holding you back. A woman in our church shared with my wife and me her journey to wholeness.

For over fifteen years of marriage, Cindy had endured abuse, neglect, and finally adultery. Her husband had abandoned her; she was raising their three small children by herself and as a result had to move into a relative's house. The pain in Cindy's life had placed the baggage of shame, worry, and disbelief in front of her future. In a desperate search for hope and healing, she had to decide whether to remain broken and hurt or to make the courageous choice of letting go of what her life had become. She was at a crisis of belief.

Cindy made the daring choice to cling to God in the midst of her heartache. As she allowed people to speak words of restoration and life into her heart, she discovered the power described in Hebrews—

> For the word of God is alive and powerful. It is sharper than the sharpest two-edged sword, cutting between soul and spirit, between joint and marrow. It exposes our innermost thoughts and desires. (Heb. 4:12 NLT)

This woman overcame the biggest test of her life to let God do His work in her heart and become the woman and mother He had called her to be. Though it was no doubt one of the hardest decisions in her life, to this day she remains grateful for making it.

Part of Cindy's transformation was linked to the fact that someone reached out and rescued her from the baggage, just as Saul experienced when he was chosen to become king of Israel.

> [Samuel said,] "Present yourselves formally before GOD, ranked in tribes and families."
>
> After Samuel got all the tribes of Israel lined up, the Benjamin tribe was picked. Then he lined up the Benjamin tribe in family groups, and the family of Matri was picked. The family of Matri took its place in the lineup, and the name Saul, son of Kish, was picked. But when they went looking for him, he was nowhere to be found.
>
> Samuel went back to GOD: "Is he anywhere around?"
>
> GOD said, "Yes, he's right over there—hidden in that pile of baggage."
>
> *They ran and got him.* He took his place before everyone, standing tall—head and shoulders above them. (1 Sam. 10:19–23 Message, emphasis added)

God will always send to you anointed and appointed people who are called to unlock your blessing and breakthrough—someone to help you become the person you're called to be. I challenge you to be open to those God has placed in your life. The Bible speaks of the protection, strength, and force of entering into the power of partnership.

Two people are better off than one, for they can help each other succeed. If one person falls, the other can reach out and help. But someone who falls alone is in real trouble. . . . A person standing alone can be attacked and defeated, but two can stand back-to-back and conquer. Three are even better, for a triple-braided cord is not easily broken. (Eccles. 4:9–10, 12 NLT)

Christian psychiatrist Paul Tournier likened the most important choices in life to a trapeze. We hold on to one trapeze bar as we swing in the air. To grab the next bar, we have to let go of the one we're holding. We can think about it for hours, we can plan the release in our minds, but we simply can't grab the new bar until we let go of the one we're holding. This image illustrates what it means to face the test of our pain. Though we may be holding on to the trapeze bar of old hurts, old fears, and old habits, we see the freedom and purpose that God wants to give us in our future. We have to take bold action: we have to let go of the old and grab the new! That's what God is asking you to do right now. Will you do it?

Let go of the old and grab the new!

In his book *The Meaning of Persons*, Tournier wrote, "The adventurous life is not one exempt from fear, but on the contrary, one that is lived in full knowledge of fears of all kinds, one in which we go forward in spite of our fears."[4]

I've known countless people who began their heart revolution hiding behind the baggage of their past. Where once baggage weighed them down and threatened to destroy their future, hope, restoration, and true transformation have now brought a future that far outweighs their past.

How about you? Will you respond today, step out from behind your baggage, and allow God to turn your heart to the person He has called you to become? Your future is worth it.

It's not just your time, it's your *turn* to grab on to the trapeze and launch out into a fresh, new start. Come on, somebody! Go for it!

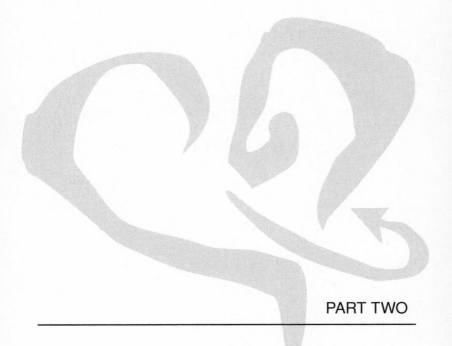

PART TWO

THE POWER BEHIND
A TURNED HEART

Watch a special video message from Pastor Sergio
Part Two: The Power behind a Turned Heart

www.sergiodelamora.com/heartrev

5

The Transforming
Power of Grace

I do not at all understand the mystery of grace—
only that it meets us where we are but does not
leave us where it found us.

—Anne Lamott, novelist

Have you ever known someone who got what they
wanted, but lost what they had?

That is the story of the prodigal son—one of the
most profound stories in the Bible. In Luke 15, Jesus tells us
about a young man who chose to live a life of instant self-
gratification. In the end, he is left with an emptiness and ache
in his heart for what he lost.

There was once a man who had two sons. The younger said to
his father, "Father, I want right now what's coming to me."
So the father divided the property between them. It wasn't
long before the younger son packed his bags and left for

a distant country. There, undisciplined and dissipated, he wasted everything he had. After he had gone through all his money, there was a bad famine all through that country and he began to hurt. (Luke 15:11–15 Message)

Though he longed to return home, he felt the sting of shame, regret, and guilt. How would he be received? How could his father forgive him for all he had done? The only way he could go home was to return, not as a son, but as a servant. He turned his heart and went back.

The miraculous power of a turned heart is vividly seen in his father's response:

So he returned home to his father. And while he was still a long way off, his father saw him coming. Filled with love and compassion, he ran to his son, embraced him, and kissed him. His son said to him, "Father, I have sinned against both heaven and you, and I am no longer worthy of being called your son."

But his father said to the servants, "Quick! Bring the finest robe in the house and put it on him. Get a ring for his finger and sandals for his feet. And kill the calf we have been fattening. We must celebrate with a feast for this son of mine was dead and has now returned to life. He was lost but now he is found." (Luke 15:20–24 NLT)

The son expected his father to meet him with accusations and judgment. Instead, he ran to him with arms open wide, covering his son, not with guilt, but with grace and unconditional love.

This is probably one of the most beautiful illustrations in the Bible of how our heavenly Father welcomes us home after we have made choices that have left us feeling undeserving and unworthy to be called a son or daughter. God Himself throws His arms open and extends to us, not judgment, but the life-transforming power of grace.

The greatest example of grace I have ever seen had its beginnings one night in my office after service. Sean and Jennifer, a beloved couple in our church, had been married for many years and had recently shared the exciting news that they were expecting another child. Our church rejoiced with them and eagerly awaited the arrival of their baby. That night, when Jennifer was nearly eight months pregnant, she came sobbing to my office with a secret that she was confident would shatter her family. She was tormented by guilt, shame, and condemnation, because the baby she was carrying

God Himself throws His arms open and extends to us the life-transforming power of grace.

was not her husband's child. Every day she lived with the pain of what she had done, and the regret was crushing her.

Through uncontrollable tears Jennifer revealed the heart-breaking secret she had been carrying for months. She cried for forgiveness, for regret, but most of all for shame. I watched Sean—a man who was well respected, well loved, and well connected—try to grasp what he had just heard. Like a ton of bricks, his world had come crashing down . . . again. He had been married before, and for years he had wrestled through his own guilt and pain to make sense of his failed first marriage. Grace had ultimately triumphed in his heart as God released to him a second chance to love and be loved. Now the woman he loved was in desperate need of the same grace that had changed his life.

Pained and devastated, Sean sat in my office, forced to make a choice. He had every right to leave Jennifer, every right to divorce her, every right to walk away. Yet this man did the unthinkable, the very opposite of what most people would have done. He forgave her, fathered this child as his own, and has never once let his wife feel the shame of her past. He liberated her through the power of grace.

You never really know if you believe in grace until you're put in a position where you must extend grace to someone who doesn't deserve it or you have a need for it to be extended to you. Jennifer got a second chance from God and from her husband, and she has never looked back. Today, the grace that freed her now gives her the confidence to help hundreds of other women understand its transforming power.

Maybe you've lived your life under someone else's judgment, and so you wrestle with the idea that you too can be free from punishment and guilt. The grace Jennifer experienced is the same grace God is extending to you.

Or maybe you're someone who has not entered into the fullness of God's grace because you simply don't believe you need it. You don't feel like you've ever done anything "that bad." You haven't experienced the hurt and brokenness others have endured—by all accounts, you have been a good person. In the story of the prodigal son, there was another son who felt just like this. He didn't leave his father or squander his inheritance. He did all the right things. But when his younger brother returned, instead of entering into the joy of his father, his heart remained bitter, angry, and jealous. He needed grace to see his brother through his father's eyes, not for his brother's benefit but for his own.

> Meanwhile, the older son was in the fields working. When he returned home, he heard music and dancing in the house, and he asked one of the servants what was going on. "Your brother is back," he was told, "and your father has killed the fattened calf. We are celebrating because of his safe return."
>
> The older brother was angry and wouldn't go in. His father came out and begged him, but he replied, "All these years I've slaved for you and never once refused to do a single thing you told me to. And in all that time you never gave me even one young goat for a feast with my friends. Yet when this son of yours comes back after squandering your money on prostitutes, you celebrate by killing the fattened calf!"
>
> His father said to him, "Look, dear son, you have always stayed by me, and everything I have is yours. We had to celebrate this happy day. For your brother was dead and has come back to life! He was lost, but now he is found!" (Luke 15:25–32 NLT)

God's grace reaches not only to those like the prodigal son who know full well of their need for mercy and grace, but also to those like the older brother who don't yet understand that they too need the freedom grace brings.

There are also those who've tried everything possible to make the "old things pass away." But nothing has stopped the old memories, the old habits, and the old mentalities from creeping back. No matter how hard they try to be good, think good, or act good, they just can't seem to stay good. So why try?

It's as if they are holding a bar of soap, and every time they blow it, instead of coming to God openly and asking Him to help them make changes in their life, they pull out the soap and try to wash away their sins. For some, the soap is their own good works. For others, it is their excuses or reasonings. In either case, there never seems to be enough soap to wash away the pain of not being able to experience the freedom that only comes from God's grace. Washing away the sins in our life with the soap of "good works" will never cure the spiritual heart disease that plagues us.

God's grace rescues us from believing the lie that we are defined by what we've done and redeems us from thinking that we must constantly pay for our mistakes. Every one of us has made decisions that need the transforming grace He is offering. It is forgiveness freely given to us—forgiveness we don't deserve—at Christ's expense. When you turn your heart and experience the wondrous power of His grace, you become a brand-new person in Christ with wholeness, vitality, and a fresh, new start!

The Heart Revolution begins with an honest assessment that our hearts need the transforming touch of God's incredible grace. Jeremiah had no illusions about the condition of the human heart prior to the revelation of God's grace:

> The heart is deceitful above all things,
> And desperately wicked;
> Who can know it? (Jer. 17:9)

And Solomon warns us,

> Guard your heart above all else,
>> for it determines the course of your life. (Prov. 4:23 NLT)

The course of a person's life will always be determined by the condition of their heart. What's the condition of your heart today? Who do you resemble in the story of the prodigal son? Are you like the younger brother, feeling far from God and desperate for change? Or are you like the older brother, who self-righteously insisted on proving that he was more acceptable because he had made better choices than his brother, thereby imposing guilt rather than expressing grace? Or are you the father, waiting for a son or daughter to leave a life of self-indulgence or spiritual darkness? Either way, listen today to the voice of the Holy Spirit, who was sent to lead us into all truth, and respond to the liberating power of God's grace. Remember, great things are on the other side of your obedience.

The course of a person's life will always be determined by the condition of their heart.

No situation is outside of God's touch. As you step out, expect great changes in your family and in your life. If you take the limits off God, He can accelerate the hope and healing you long to see. I challenge you now to pick up the phone, write the email, send the text, or make the visit!

As Malachi said in the last verse of the Old Testament,

> And he [God] will turn
>> The hearts of the fathers to the children,
>> And the hearts of the children to their fathers.
> (4:6)

6

Revolutionizing Your Beliefs

> God has no religion.
> —Mahatma Ghandi

Over years of pastoring I have come to the conclusion that the biggest roadblock to a real relationship with God is religion. Many people believe religion and relationship are synonymous, but this misconception often hinders people from entering a legitimate relationship with God and experiencing genuine change.

Religion is our attempt to reach God by our own efforts, to do enough good deeds so that we gain acceptance and admittance into heaven. A legitimate *relationship* with God is birthed from a heart that has been melted and molded by grace and now longs to please Him more than ever—not to prove ourselves or earn points with God, but to honor the One who loves us so much that He was willing to die for us.

The beauty of a genuine relationship with Christ is that we gain access to the full gamut of Christ's nature and character, whereas religion will cause us to operate out of an incomplete and false image of God.

Everyone has an image of Christ in their minds that determines how they will approach and respond to Him. For some, their image is that of a gentle Shepherd tending to His sheep. For others, He is an elusive deity to whom they simply cannot relate. For still others, their image is that of a bleeding, crucified Savior, still on the cross, who's been stripped of power and authority. The problem with all of these images is that they give an inaccurate and incomplete picture of Christ. Take, for example, the image of a crucified Savior, still on the cross for the sins of the world. A person with this image in the forefront of their mind may feel as if they have to ask repeatedly for forgiveness of their sins. The problem with this image is that Jesus is no longer on the cross!

In a rule-driven society, many people strive to measure up in life so they can be labeled as accepted and successful. Some of us naturally gravitate toward rules because we can see obvious progress, and we can measure ourselves against others. This is a very "religious" approach to life. If we aren't doing as well as others, we can try a little harder; if we're doing better than our competitors, we can feel proud of ourselves. The problem with this perspective is that, though measuring sticks give us a sense of security, they will never substitute for the liberation and acceptance that come from a relationship with the living God.

As a son, father, and pastor, I have felt the weight of pressure that comes from trying to measure up to the standards and perceptions of others. In the beginning days of Cornerstone Church—before we had a building, before we had people lining up for the next service, before we had more than one service—I remember hearing the doubts of other people. They would tell me, "You're never going to be able to set up and break down every week." I remember sitting in a green plastic chair before service at Hilltop High School and praying, "God, I can't do this without You. People are going to come to Your house today and they need to know You love them despite their mistakes. They didn't come to hear the voice of a man. Help them hear Your voice today, God." Keeping my focus on God and His work liberated me from thinking about the expectations of others.

A relationship with Jesus will always lead to an "I can" on the inside of you, whereas religion will always focus on an "I can't!" God

A relationship with Jesus will always lead to an "I can" on the inside of you.

is not interested in measuring our mistakes and successes; He just wants to know if we'll believe in Him and stay connected to Him through a genuine personal relationship with His Son.

When religion replaces a genuine relationship with Christ, we venture down a road that denies us the very power that God longs for us to have. In a letter to Timothy, Paul warns,

> You should know this, Timothy, that in the last days there will be very difficult times. . . . [For people] will act religious, but they will reject the power that could make them godly. (2 Tim. 3:1, 5 NLT)

The power to turn our hearts and change the trajectory of our lives cannot be obtained through religion, because religion lacks the inherent power to change the condition of our hearts:

- Relationship draws us into life transformation; religion drives us into self-improvement.
- Relationship allows us to tap into God's liberating power over sin and death; religion causes us to profess a power we haven't truly possessed.
- Relationship gives us God's perspective for the hurting and unsaved; religion causes us to criticize and condemn those God wants to cleanse and heal.

Living religiously leads to frustration, as we see in Acts 19. The miraculous evidence of Paul's relationship with Jesus Christ prompted others to look for the miraculous as well. However, without the authenticity of truly knowing Christ, certain men were unable to call on Christ to expel demons:

> Some Jews who went around driving out evil spirits tried to invoke the name of the Lord Jesus over those who were demon-possessed. They would say, "In the name of Jesus, whom Paul preaches, I command you to come out." . . . (One day) the evil spirit answered them, "Jesus I know, and I know about Paul, but who are you?" (Acts 19:13, 15 NIV)

They couldn't live in the power of God's grace because they hadn't experienced it. They couldn't bring healing to others because they didn't know the Healer. They had heard of the one Paul preached about but had yet to know Him intimately. There is a difference between knowing Christ up close, as Paul did, and knowing Christ from a distance, as these men did. No matter what you've known about God in the past, you have been called to know God and His healing power up close and personal!

Most people I have counseled over the years have walked away from God not because they wanted to but because they felt as though they just couldn't measure up to the rules and regulations that often define religion.

Many years ago, before we even had a facility, I began a television broadcast in an effort to bring people to our grand opening happening in the upcoming weeks. One day I was sitting in my office, and the phone rang. When I answered, a deep, raspy voice on the other end asked, "Are you Pastor Sergio?" I took a deep breath and said, "Yes." The man told me he had watched our television broadcast the night before. Then with obvious pain and regret, he began to share his past with me. John had been a gangbanger most of his life and had committed some of the most heinous crimes imaginable.

He confessed he was still in a gang that was notorious for being the most violent in Southern California.

He spoke about how other members of his gang had been murdered by his own hand for trying to get out of gang life. John's tired voice painted a picture in my mind of a man aged far beyond his years because of the life he had lived. He wanted to get out of the gang; that much I could tell by the desperation in his voice. But at every point when I heard a breaking in his deep, strained voice, he would revert back to the steely, calm words, "I'm not calling for me, Pastor. I'm calling because I need your help." When I asked John how I could help, his voice finally broke. It took him a moment before he regained his composure and said, "Pastor, can you help get my family to heaven? I know I can never be forgiven for what I've done, but will you help them?"

His voice had penetrated my heart, and I knew without a shadow of a doubt that God had orchestrated this call. What I learned during the rest of that conversation was that John was calling from a federal penitentiary where he was serving consecutive life sentences. I assured him that I would do my best to reach out to his family, and then slowly I began to explain to him that God's plan for salvation included him as well. John half laughed and said flatly, "Pastor, people like me don't get forgiven. I've done too many things wrong to be forgiven. I believe God can help my family, but I can't be helped anymore."

My heart broke to hear he had hope for his family but only despair for himself. For the next thirty minutes he explained to me why he believed the crimes he had committed and the lifestyle he had chosen disqualified him from ever being forgiven. My eyes teared up as he said, "God could never let someone like me into heaven." I was so moved that my hands shook as he begged me to reach out to his young kids so that they didn't follow in his footsteps.

John's belief system wouldn't allow him to consider the possibility that he could be forgiven for the crimes he had committed. His mindset wouldn't let him see beyond his sin to experience the incredible love and grace Christ offered. It was one of the most gut-wrenching conversations I've ever had. I couldn't just hang up the phone and walk away. I was committed to him, to his family, and to his future. Many people would have laughed at the far-fetched idea that this man still had a future, but I was not giving up without a fight.

For the next two years I spent time with him over the phone, challenging his beliefs about the depth of God's love for him. Some days were harder than others. Some were better. It was bittersweet for me, because I never knew what happened after the line went dead—if he thought about our conversations as much as I did or not. I never knew if he'd call again. I just had to be ready if he decided to reach out.

John never did walk through the doors of my church, but salvation reached out beyond our walls to meet him where he was. I went to the prison he called home, and both of us grown men cried as he prayed the prayer of salvation. Sometime later I had the privilege of leading his children to salvation as well. Though he never set foot outside prison, a genuine relationship with Christ had given him a freedom that no one could ever take away.

Like John's experience, the greatest ache in humanity is that of needing to bridge the gap between religion and genuine relationship with God. God's love for you reaches beyond religion to give you permission to come boldly into His presence. You are His son or daughter, and the deepest desire of His heart is for you to know His love, His grace, His forgiveness!

God can revolutionize any belief and rebuild any foundation. If all you've known is religion, start today to build a relationship with Him that assures you of His infinite love for you.

7

The Supremacy of Christ

The greatest enemy of Christianity may be people
who say they believe in Jesus but who are no longer
astonished and amazed.

—Mike Yaconelli, cofounder,
Youth Specialties

There is no circumstance or situation we could ever face that Jesus himself did not face and overcome while he was on earth. He was tempted, ridiculed, betrayed, and misunderstood so that he could transfer to us the liberating power to overcome when we are tempted, ridiculed, betrayed, and misunderstood. Jesus transferred to you and me the power to go from conquered to conqueror and overcome to overcomer when he said,

Behold, I give you the authority to trample on serpents and
scorpions, and over all the power of the enemy, and nothing
shall by any means hurt you. (Luke 10:19)

This is the core reason why a single mother can find the hope and power to rise above hurt and betrayal, or why a drug addict can find the strength to stand against and overcome the temptation of another fix, or why a workaholic can find the courage to discover they have more value than their paycheck. They have found God's grace and thereby the power and authority in Jesus Christ to get up! They have found His supremacy triumphs over their humanity. Today it is my prayer that, as you walk in the fullness of His forgiveness for you, you would also discover the greatness of His power that now lives in you!

My prayer is that you would discover the greatness of God's power that lives in you!

Most people today often feel powerless to get up from the weight of debt they carry every day—debt that is both emotional and financial. Credit card debt has skyrocketed in recent years, and many families carry this burden on top of mortgages, car loans, and other unsecured loans. Even more often, these visible debts are compounded by the deep and oppressive emotional debts people carry in their hearts. Every sin, every disappointment, and every heartache creates a debt in their hearts. It was this debt that broke Jesus' heart when He looked out at the multitudes and saw their weight of loneliness and weariness (Matt. 9:36). And it was this debt that drove Him to the cross, the only place He could pay for humanity's sins and fully demonstrate His power over all things, even death.

Many years ago, I met a man named Rick who needed these words more than anything else in the world. He had gotten lost in a sea of alcohol, sex, and pornography as a teenager, failed in college, and ended up alone and depressed as an adult. Rick drifted in and out of relationships and careers for years, longing to find the elusive feeling of genuine success and achievement. But it never came. Every time he failed, he heard the words of his disappointed parents, "You're a failure. You'll never make it now. You've failed too many times. You're just not good enough, Rick." His father's face of frustration and anger haunted him in every venture until eventually he just stopped trying.

The day I met Rick, I saw a man locked behind years of pain, who was tired of losing, tired of failing, and tired of feeling worthless. He never smiled or laughed and spoke only when necessary. He was like a walking corpse, a prisoner to his past identity and mistakes, and no matter how hard he tried, he couldn't break free. He was bound by the pain of rejection and regret. For weeks, he came with his girlfriend to church like that . . .

Until one day he found the courage to take brave steps toward the altar and give his life to Christ. I looked him straight in the eyes and began to tell him, "You aren't powerless, you aren't defeated, you aren't a failure." These words fell on the deadness of his heart and began to break up the soil of lie after lie and mistake after mistake. Rick began to weep as Jesus poured into him forgiveness, hope, and strength. Later he shared with me that during that season of transformation, he stood on the words of the prophet Isaiah,

> He gives power to the weak
>> and strength to the powerless.
> Even youths will become weak and tired,
>> and young men will fall in exhaustion.
> But those who trust in the LORD will find new
>> strength. (Isa. 40:29–31 NLT)

The Holy Spirit's power over the voice of condemnation that Rick had wrestled with for years had not only liberated him but had given him the courage to get up and pursue the true desires of his heart. Did he ever feel the sting of failure again? Yes, many times. But he now had inside him the unlimited power and strength to get up and stay up!

Rick's experience is what Paul was describing when he compared a person's condition to a Roman debtor's prison. In his day, when someone couldn't pay his debts, he was put in a cell, and a list of his debts was tacked over his cell door for all to see. Paul wrote to the believers in Colossae,

> And with him you were raised to new life because you trusted the mighty power of God, who raised Christ from the dead. You were dead because of your sins and because your sinful nature was not yet cut away. Then God made you alive with Christ, for he forgave all our sins. He canceled the record of the charges against us and took it away by nailing it to the cross. (Col. 2:13–14 NLT)

The list of debts was "against" us because it kept us locked in prison. But Jesus took our list and nailed it to His cell door, the cross. His commitment to rescuing lost people and redeeming a fallen world had reached fulfillment when He uttered His last words on the cross, "It is finished," and our list of debts was stamped "Paid in Full." When we say, "We're free," we aren't saying that our freedom is free. We are saying we understand that our freedom from debts cost the Son of God His life. But the list doesn't cover just the past debts of sins we've said, done, and thought. The list Christ paid for includes every sin for the rest of our lives until we see Him face-to-face. Everything . . . all of it . . . no exceptions. It's amazing!

Jesus took our list and nailed it to His cell door, the cross.

This is why today Jesus doesn't want you to just read about who He is. He wants you to know Him personally so that you can experience freedom in ways you never thought possible. Even more amazing is the fact that Christ didn't just free us and leave us on our own. In a wonderful extension of His grace, He welcomes us into the family of God and adopts us as His own! We are sons and daughters of the King, with the privilege to approach the throne at any time with anything on our minds.

As we draw closer to Him and become more intimate with Him, we must constantly keep a sense of wonder and amazement about Christ so that we don't become overfamiliar. Though He has become approachable, we must never lose sight that we are approaching Almighty God. Professor and author J. I. Packer has observed:

> Today, vast stress is laid on the thought that God is personal, but this truth is so stated as to leave the impression that God is a person of the same sort we are. . . . But this is not the God of the Bible! Our personal life is a finite thing: it is limited in every direction, in space, in time, in knowledge, in power. But God is not so limited. He is eternal, infinite, and almighty. He has us in His hands; but we never have Him in ours. Like us, He is personal, but unlike us He is great. In all its constant stress on the reality of God's personal concern for His people, and on the gentleness, tenderness, sympathy, patience, and yearning compassion that He shows towards them, the Bible never lets us lose sight of His majesty, and His unlimited dominion over all His creatures.[5]

Wonder at the greatness of God and a sense of Christ's supremacy are essential elements to genuine faith. It's this revelation of His magnificence and radiance that causes us to pause and reflect during prayer rather than rush through. It's what keeps our hearts mesmerized and amazed that He claims us as His friends.

I challenge you to close your eyes and ask God to give you a greater perspective of who you have living inside you! Ask Him to reveal to you His supremacy, authority, and dominion over all that you may be struggling with today. If you don't know the words to say, pray this prayer with me:

Dear Jesus,

Help me today to have a deeper understanding of who You are in my life. Help me to see that You are greater than what I'm going through and that everything I need is in You. I need Your strength today to see my life through the great price You paid at the cross so that I will never doubt Your power to help me overcome any situation. Your grace covers me today and gives me the authority and ability to declare that I am not what I've done and I'm not who I used to be! Thank You for increasing my faith for the unimaginable, because I serve the God of more than enough!

In Jesus' name, Amen.

Delve into God's amazing goodness and purposes for your life and discover the value and worth that is inside you. Allow your heart to be adopted into His family so that you may realize the power and authority He has given you as His own son or daughter. Begin to believe He has plans that are far bigger and deeper than anything you could ever imagine.

Today is your day to begin to do amazing things for Him and His kingdom so the world may know by your testimony that they can get up too.

8

You and the Holy Spirit

If we think of the Holy Spirit only as an impersonal power or influence, then our thought will constantly be, "How can I get hold of and use the Holy Spirit?"; but if we think of Him in the biblical way as a divine Person, infinitely wise, infinitely holy, infinitely tender, then our thought will constantly be, "How can the Holy Spirit get hold of and use me?"

—Reuben Archer Torrey, evangelist

There will come a moment in the walk of every believer when God will ask you to get to know another part of Himself. This chapter emphasizes the importance of the Holy Spirit, because many times the Holy Spirit is the most neglected person of the Trinity. In the last conversation Jesus had with His disciples before His arrest, He told them that the Holy Spirit would come to be with them after He was gone.

> These things I have spoken to you while being present with you. But the Helper, the Holy Spirit, whom the Father will send in My name, He will teach you all things, and bring to your remembrance all things that I said to you. (John 14:25–26)

And He explained the role of the Holy Spirit:

> It is to your advantage that I go away; for if I do not go away, the Helper will not come to you; but if I depart, I will send Him to you. And when He has come, He will convict the world of sin, and of righteousness, and of judgment: of sin, because they do not believe in Me; of righteousness, because I go to My Father and you see Me no more; of judgment, because the ruler of this world is judged. (John 16:7–11)

Jesus didn't leave us on our own to try to do His will. When we become believers, the Holy Spirit comes into our lives and inhabits our hearts. Oftentimes many people wonder if the Holy Spirit is simply just an ambiguous or impersonal force. Yet the Bible tells us He is a person equal in every way with God the Father and God the Son. He is the third member of the Godhead. Jesus' great commission to the disciples reveals the unity of the three:

Many times the Holy Spirit is the most neglected person of the Trinity.

> All authority has been given to Me in heaven and on earth. Go therefore and make disciples of all the nations, baptizing them in the name of the Father and of the Son and of the Holy Spirit, teaching them to observe all things that I have commanded you. (Matt. 28:18–20)

God is Father, Son, and Holy Spirit. And all the divine attributes credited to the Father and the Son are equally given to the Holy Spirit. The Bible gives us powerful insight into the character and divine nature of the Holy Spirit. He has intellect, emotion, and will (see 1 Cor. 12:11; Rom. 15:30). Before Christ, the presence of God dwelled in the temple in Jerusalem; now God dwells in the hearts of every believer through the Holy Spirit.

As you come to know the Holy Spirit more personally, you will see that He will do what Jesus promised He would do: lead you, help you grasp truth, use you to lead people to Christ, and equip and empower you to serve God in every aspect of life. I encourage you to stay open to the ministry of the Holy Spirit in your life today. He is here to help you and guide you and produce God's character in your life. When you feel lacking in such attributes of God as peace, love, and joy, it is the Holy Spirit who goes to work inside you to cultivate these things in you.

> But the fruit of the Spirit is love, joy, peace, longsuffering, kindness, goodness, faithfulness, gentleness, self-control. (Gal. 5:22–23)

Consider how Jesus' words read in the Amplified Bible:

> And I will ask the Father, and He will give you another Comforter (Counselor, Helper, Intercessor, Advocate, Strengthener, and Standby), that He may remain with you forever. (John 14:16)

The Holy Spirit was sent to us for our benefit! He becomes all of these incredible things for us when we welcome Him into our hearts. Let these words fall fresh on your heart today: you have a Comforter, Counselor, Helper, Intercessor, Advocate, and Strengthener inside you who will never leave you. The Holy Spirit even helps you when you don't know how or what to pray for. Paul writes,

> Likewise the Spirit also helps in our weaknesses. For we do not know what we should pray for as we ought, but the Spirit

Himself makes intercession for us with groanings which cannot be uttered. Now He who searches the hearts knows what the mind of the Spirit is, because He makes intercession for the saints according to the will of God. (Rom. 8:26–27)

When the Holy Spirit dwells in you, it is God's "seal" on your life that acts as a guarantee of your inheritance (Eph. 1:13–14). The Holy Spirit acts as the power source in the life of every believer. It's the Holy Spirit who brings fresh revelation and wisdom (Eph. 1:17–18). It's the Holy Spirit who brings a fresh boldness to witness to others around us (1 Tim. 3:13). It's the Holy Spirit who gives us the power to live this revolutionary life (Ezek. 36:27). And it's the Holy Spirit who baptizes us with fire and passion by evidence of speaking in other tongues (Acts 1:8; 2:4).

The Holy Spirit is the battery in your walk with Christ.

Allow God today to bring new things into your life through the Holy Spirit. Let go of any preconceived idea about what you may have been told about Him. Welcome Him into your heart so He can share with you the secrets of the Father, intercede on your behalf, and give you the gift and power to live a revolutionary life. He is the battery in your walk with Christ, keeping the passion and energy for God active and alive!

Many times the world doesn't understand the power and purposes of the Holy Spirit, and as a result many churches today pull back from embracing a relationship with Him. Many Christians shy away from saying that they are Spirit-filled because they fear being misunderstood or maybe because they simply feel like they don't have enough understanding of how the Holy Spirit works in their life.

Many years ago a man came up to me and said, "Pastor Sergio, I love Jesus and I want to follow Him, but I'm still not convinced about the Holy Spirit. I'm not sure He really exists." I gave him a challenge that he later told me changed everything about his relationship with the Holy Spirit. I looked him in the eye and said, "Don't try to convince yourself that He exists. Try convincing yourself that He doesn't exist." He looked at me as if I had just told him the craziest thing he'd ever heard. Prove that there was no Holy Spirit? He went home that day and began to read every Scripture he could find to prove that the Holy Spirit was not real. In his search to disprove the Holy Spirit's existence, he found countless evidence that the Holy Spirit was in fact real. And in looking for hours, days, and even weeks, he had not only convinced himself the Holy Spirit was real, but he couldn't live without Him! Scripture after Scripture about the nature, divinity, and power of the Holy Spirit had set his heart on fire for God. He came to me weeks later and said, "I give up! He's real. And more than that, I found a Friend I never knew I needed."

I challenge you to ask God to reveal who the Holy Spirit is in your life. I know if you will expand your faith to know the Holy Spirit, you, like this man, will discover a friend you never knew you needed. I pray you would tap into the power that lives inside you today. Tap into the power of the Holy Spirit who has the ability to take your life to another dimension! Or as my friend Ed Young says, "It's time to go to an HNL—a wHole 'Nother Level!"

Come on, somebody! Let's go!

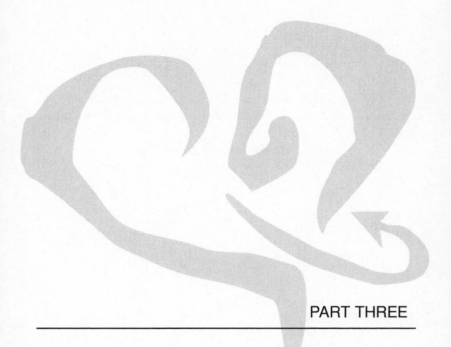

RISKS AND REWARDS OF JOINING THE REVOLUTION

Watch a special video message from Pastor Sergio
Part Three: Risks and Rewards of Joining the Revolution

www.sergiodelamora.com/heartrev

9

There's No Victory
without Risk

To love is to risk not being loved in return. To
hope is to risk pain. To try is to risk failure, but
risk must be taken because the greatest hazard in
life is to risk nothing.

—Anonymous

It's one thing when a family moves to an unknown city with
the security of a job and a home. It's something else entirely when a family moves to an unknown city without any
security at all. This is exactly what my family did. My wife,
Georgina, who was seven months pregnant at the time, and
I packed up our children and left the comforts of everything
we had ever known—our family, our business, our church,
our friends. There were no guarantees, and at times, the risks
of starting a church in a city of people who had no idea who

we were was overwhelming, but we pressed through because we knew God had called us. I remember sitting with an open telephone book on my lap, asking God, "Why do we need to go to San Diego? Look at all these churches, God. There's so many! Why do we need to go there?" At the time we had no idea that our mission statement "To turn the hearts of youth and families to God and to each other" would start a revolution. All we knew was that God was commissioning us that day as I flipped through the Yellow Pages. He said, "Sergio, if they were doing what I need you to do, I wouldn't be sending you." His words were enough for us to leave everything and take the risk of starting Cornerstone Church of San Diego.

Perhaps it was because I was introduced to the language of risk taking at a young age that fear didn't hinder my steps as an adult. My parents had modeled for me countless times the risks required to be successful in life. My father, though he spoke only limited English, refused to let anything stop him from becoming a successful entrepreneur. He once told me, "Nothing can stop you from becoming the best, except yourself." He constantly chose to pursue the best clients and take on the largest projects, despite the risk of being embarrassed by the language barrier.

I'll never forget the day my father taught me a great lesson about risk. I was fifteen years old and I was on a landscaping job with my dad when he told me to trim the branches on the tallest tree I'd ever seen in my life. I remember standing at the base of that forty-foot Stone Pine tree, looking up at branches that seemed tall enough to graze the clouds, thinking, "My father is trying to kill me. He has other sons. He doesn't care if something happens to me." My dad grabbed the tallest ladder we had, steadied it against the tree, and held it in place as I took my first step. As I climbed higher and higher, I kept sneaking looks down to see if he would change his mind and call me back down. He didn't. He waited at the bottom of the tree, never once letting go of the ladder until I finished my task and made it safely back down. When the soles of my feet hit the dirt, my dad looked at me and said, "You must always risk in order to go farther than you thought you could and achieve what you thought was impossible."

God is saying the same thing to you. He's holding your ladder so that you can reach for things that have been out of your reach and pursue the unattainable. He issues a challenge to us:

> Call to Me, and I will answer you, and show you great and mighty things, which you do not know. (Jer. 33:3)

Risk is important to God because it demonstrates to Him our commitment to go after the things we really want. Even over two thousand years ago, the men and women who walked with Jesus were under no illusions about the risks and rewards of following Him. They had watched some of the most dramatic, amazing things eyes have ever seen: the lame walked, the blind could see, the sick were healed, the dead came back to life, and the sea became calm at Christ's command. At the pinnacle of Jesus' ministry, the rewards were unimaginable. Yet the risks were often just as great. Time after time, religious leaders argued with Him, rejected Him, and eventually turned Him over to the Romans to be killed. At the end of His life, the risks proved to be more than His disciples could handle. The night before His arrest, they ran because they were terrified that they too would be arrested, whipped, and murdered. But the book of Acts tells us they chose to follow Jesus after His death, gathering to wait for the promise He had given them, in spite of the threat of imprisonment or worse. Risks and rewards weren't vague concepts to them. Yet they were convinced that following Jesus was the greatest adventure life has ever known.

Maybe up until now your life never had anything worth risking for. Or maybe you're afraid to risk again because you've been disappointed too many times in the past. Maybe you've found yourself at a place where you've risked everything you had and now there's simply nothing left.

A woman I met many years ago felt just like that. I first heard Lisa's name when one of her family members asked me to pray for her. She had tried to commit suicide, and her family didn't know if she would pull through. Lisa had grown up watching her parents struggle with alcohol, adultery, and violence until ultimately it became too dangerous for her and her siblings to live at home. To escape the pain she had carried, Lisa did what many women from these families do: she repeated the cycle and entered into destructive relationships that left her alone and rejected over and over again. Every night she would bury her face into her pillow and cry out, "Why doesn't anyone want me? What is so horrible about me that no one can love me?" She would have taken the love of anyone over the gnawing ache of loneliness that she carried in her heart every day. And that's exactly what she did.

She married a man who abused her mentally, physically, emotionally, and sexually. No matter how bad it got, Lisa was determined not to be alone again. For over two long, brutal years, she endured abuse until one day he threatened to leave her. It should have been liberating, but like many other abused people, Lisa was so hurt and desperate to feel loved and accepted, she begged him to stay with her. She threatened him, "If you leave me, I'll kill myself." Her threats didn't move him. As he walked toward the door, she went to the kitchen, found a sharp knife, and began cutting her arms and wrists. He looked back at her one final time before walking out of the house. When her roommate came home, she found Lisa lying on the floor, bleeding. By the time the ambulance came, she had slipped into a coma. She had lost her will to live.

Three thousand miles away, my phone rang, and I was asked to pray and intercede for Lisa. Her family rushed to her side, and after a few days, she came out of the coma and slowly began to recover. Her family filled her hospital room with worship, praying for a miracle. As she began to heal physically, she reached out to God and begged Him to love her and give her a second chance. Eventually, she was released from the hospital and the following Sunday, she walked through the doors of Cornerstone Church. Lisa sat quietly in her chair and listened to every word of hope I spoke. After the message, I looked at her and said, "I've been praying for you, Lisa." As tears poured down her cheeks, I told her, "It doesn't matter what you've done or what you've been through. Your new life has started." This young woman, shattered by pain and rejection, found love, acceptance, and peace in Christ. In the years since that day, Lisa has been a beacon of hope to every person she meets. Whenever I need to be reminded what the Heart Revolution is about, I think of her story. God revolutionized her with His unwavering love, and she chooses now to be a revolutionary for thousands of others.

If Lisa had been too cautious or too afraid, or if she'd used any other excuse for turning down God's hand in her time of need, she would have missed it all. Today, she says, "All traces of my past life are distant memories." She has a loving husband, wonderful children, and a look on her face that says, "The risk of reaching out to Christ was well worth it. The rewards of turning my heart and joining the Heart Revolution far outweigh any risks."

Like Lisa, everyone comes to a moment in life where they face the risk of doing what they've never done to become what they've never been.

This is that moment for you.

Someone once said, "Don't be afraid to go out on a limb. That's where the fruit is." As you step out today and begin to take risks for God, I believe fruit is coming into your life like you've never seen before—fruit that will allow you to love again, believe again, and forgive again.

10

The Rewards of Opening Your Heart

The purpose of life is to live it, to taste experience to the utmost, to reach out eagerly and without fear for newer and richer experience.

—Eleanor Roosevelt

One of the ministerial moments I will never forget came in the spring of 2010 when I had the incredible opportunity to visit several orphanages in Haiti with Ed Young Jr. and C3 Global after the 7.0 earthquake that devastated most of the nation. Before I left, many people warned me of the risks of traveling to such an undeveloped country, risks that threatened my health and safety. If I had been too afraid of the danger involved, I never would have entered into the joy of opening my heart to a nation that so desperately needs hope and healing. If I had been content to watch it from my television or read about it in the newspaper, I never would have played, laughed, and prayed with children who are so much like mine. If I had left the risk for someone else to brave, I would have missed the reward of waves of compassion pouring into my heart for a people who have endured tragedy yet remain hopeful.

I saw the dangers. I saw the rows and rows of tents that rested over a graveyard of thousands. I saw the risks. But I also saw the

Rewards cause a person to see the risk but pursue the reward anyway.

hope of renewal, of restoration, and of life again. I pray that your eyes and heart would see the same today. Perhaps you see the dangers and risks of moving forward and believing for greater things. I pray that you would focus on the rewards. How much would you risk to see the reward of your marriage restored? Or your children come home? Or your family healed? Or your business revived? These are the rewards that cause a person to see the risk but pursue the reward anyway.

Today I want to share with you three rewards that you and I can be confident of as we open our hearts to God.

The Reward of Restoration

Our God is the God of restoration. Nothing moved Him to step out of heaven, leave His throne, and become flesh, except the plight of humankind.

> And God looked upon the world and saw how degenerate, debased, and vicious it was, for all humanity had corrupted their way upon the earth and lost their true direction. (Gen. 6:12 AMP)

When all of humanity had lost everything, including their relationship with Him, God stepped in, not with judgment or condemnation, but with restoration on His mind. God doesn't shrink back from us in times of loss; He reaches out. In His limitless love, He longs for us to recover what we've lost. We may hear the daunting voice of condemnation telling us we've gone too far or that our situation is beyond repair, but you need to know, without a shadow of doubt, nothing is beyond the scope of His restoration. Nowhere is too far for Him to reach. It is this truth, confirmed through Scripture, that gives you the courage to expose the deepest parts of your loss to Him.

> GOD, your GOD, will restore everything you lost; he'll have compassion on you; he'll come back and pick up the pieces from all the places where you were scattered. No matter how far away you end up, GOD, your GOD, will get you out of there and bring you back. (Deut. 30:3–5 Message)

Think of the man with the withered hand who stood before Jesus and took the greatest risk of his life to expose that which he had kept hidden for years. Think of the risk he faced by exposing to the world his deformity, his handicap, and his weakness when Jesus told him, "Stretch out your hand" (Luke 6:8–11). I imagine there was a voice in the back of his mind that wondered, *What if Jesus doesn't heal me? What if I expose this part of my life and nothing changes?* We've all heard that voice. This man stood to his feet and risked it all—humiliation, ridicule, vulnerability—to receive his restoration. As he stepped out and risked his reputation, it was right there that he received his reward. He was completely restored.

What is withered or broken in your life? What would it look like to show this to Jesus? If you take the risk of showing your brokenness to Jesus, you will experience one of the greatest rewards you could ever imagine—complete restoration. He wants you to face every day with a freedom that comes from being completely restored. Know today with confidence that the reward of restoration will always outshine, outweigh, and outlast the sting of risking it all.

The Reward of God's Best

God's definition of His best for you is an ongoing state of success and well-being that overflows into every area of your life. Consider the well-known words of the prophet Jeremiah:

> "For I know the plans I have for you," declares the LORD, "plans to prosper you and not to harm you, plans to give you hope and a future." (Jer. 29:11 NIV)

The word "prosper" in Hebrew is the word *shalom*, which typically means peace. However, the *Theological Wordbook of the Old Testament* also lists the following definitions: "completeness, wholeness, harmony, fulfillment . . . unimpaired relationships with others and with God." This is the richness of life that Jesus risked His life for! It's the fullness that the writer of the Third Epistle of John prays for:

> Beloved, I pray that you may prosper in all things and be in health, just as your soul prospers. (3 John 2)

The text clearly conveys to us that his prayer was for God's best to overflow into all things. What is included in "all things"? Everything. Jesus made clear that part of His purpose was not just to restore that which was stolen from us but also to bring a life overflowing with good things to us. Consider His words:

> The thief comes only in order to steal and kill and destroy. I came that they may have and enjoy life, and have it in abundance (to the full, till it overflows). (John 10:10 AMP)

It has always been in the heart of God to see us blessed. Like a parent who wants to see their children succeed, so does our Father want us to live a rich, fruitful life. Your success brings joy to the Father! He risked His life for us so that we would overflow in every area. Believe with me today that success is in your future, because our God overflows with good things that He desires to give to His children. He has called you to thrive, not just survive!

The Reward of Seeing the Miraculous

Step out in risk, and you step into the realm of the miraculous. There came a day when we as a church had to step out and purchase a facility. A realtor suggested a local movie theater as a possibility. It wasn't even for sale, but my wife and I felt God prompting us to take the risk. The theater was located in the middle of a shopping plaza, and the idea of putting a non-retail business in such a prime location was met with hesitation and even hostility. I never dreamed our risk would attract so many people to our church, but it did. Those with financial interest came. Those with media interest came. Those with political interest came. They all came from the north, south, east, and west to see what was happening in a city that was once labeled forgotten and forsaken.

God has called you to thrive, not just survive!

God's promise of a permanent home gave us the courage to plow ahead on the nine-month journey with the city and pursue the purchase of the movie theater for our church. I still remember driving into the parking lot of the City Hall with Georgina and my kids, knowing that this meeting would determine our church's future. Seeing the parking lot packed to capacity with cars bearing our Cornerstone Church bumper sticker increased my faith for our future like nothing else could! That night we needed the favor of God. The council's vote would determine if our church would finally have a place to call home. Our families needed a yes. Those three little letters had never meant more to us. I stood in front of the city council members that night and poured out my heart on behalf of every family of Cornerstone Church, including mine. I gave them every reason possible why it would be the best decision for the city to vote in our favor. And when it was time to vote, it was unanimous—every single member of the council voted yes! It felt as though God had stopped all of heaven for us to declare His yes over our future. Never before in the history of our church had a reward so far outweighed the risk. That yes opened the door for over five thousand people to worship there today!

Following Christ will always have its risks, but as you begin to live with expectancy for the rewards He promised—first and foremost being a rich relationship with Him—you begin to push through any potential risks, facing them head on with the confidence to know your reward awaits you. The glory of the gospel is that God never leaves us to face any risks alone, and He never gives up on us. I've known thousands of people who said yes to Christ, fell down, and then took the risk to get up and try again because the rewards surpassed the risks.

Don't allow the risks to hold you back from stepping out for Christ. Open your heart today and let God speak to you in a powerful way. The rewards of restoration, prosperity, and the miraculous await you!

11

Finding Hope and Healing

Not only do we not know God except through Jesus Christ; we do not even know ourselves except through Jesus Christ.

—Blaise Pascal

During World War II, German bombs destroyed the beautiful and ancient stained glass in an English cathedral. As they swept up the tiny pieces of glass and looked at the hole in the wall, the people of the church were heartbroken. But someone had an idea. They asked skilled craftsmen to use the piles of shattered glass as the raw ingredients for a new window. Today, the window is a spectacular representation of what happens when we choose to use the leftovers of a devastating loss to create something new and beautiful.

God does exactly the same thing in our lives. He takes the shattered remains of our lives and creates something new, something beautiful, and something that causes people to marvel when they see it. No one is beyond God's creative powers of restoration. The Bible says that when God made the universe, He created all that exists out of nothing. If He can do that, He can use broken and discarded pieces of our lives to make something fantastically beautiful.

No one is beyond God's creative powers of restoration.

In the story of Nehemiah, the wall of Jerusalem had been torn down and burned. The wall represented a protection for the city, and without it, the people of Jerusalem were vulnerable to attacks from enemies. Nehemiah led the people to begin to rebuild the wall, but as they did, their enemy began to taunt them:

> But it so happened, when Sanballat heard that we were rebuilding the wall, that he was furious and very indignant, and mocked the Jews. And he spoke before his brethren and the army of Samaria, and said, "What are these feeble Jews doing? Will they fortify themselves? Will they offer sacrifices? Will they complete it in a day? Will they revive the stones from the heaps of rubbish—*stones* that are burned?" (Neh. 4:1–2)

Nehemiah led the people of Jerusalem to push forward, rebuild the wall, and defeat the work of their enemies.

Today the wall of Nehemiah can be seen as an allegory for our hearts. Maybe you feel like your heart has been torn down and burned by situations in your life. Maybe today you feel like all that's left is burnt stones and wonder how you could ever rebuild your life. Just as Nehemiah took the burnt stones and rebuilt the wall, God wants you to know He can and will take the burnt areas of your heart and rebuild your life!

But how? How does God put broken or burnt pieces back together? Here are some ways He crafts a new life for us.

A Renewed Mind

Our lives are the product of our beliefs and behaviors. Legitimate transformation on a heart level will always require a transformation on a mental level. Paul explained how we begin to see transformation occur from the inside out:

> Don't copy the behavior and customs of this world, but let God transform you into a new person by changing the way you think. (Rom. 12:2 NLT)

God will change the way we view and process the world around us, if we will let Him. By spending time with Him and in His Word, we begin to think radically different. When we discover the amazing things He thinks about us in His Word, we begin to view our life through His filter of hope, faith, and expectancy. That's why I encourage our church to read the *One Year Bible*. Spending time in the Word of God gives us the tools we need to avoid focusing on negative thoughts. His promises give us the ability to think positively about any situation that may come our way. Renewing our minds is vital to living a revolutionary life. When you are faced with a tough situation, instead of looking at it the way you may have in the past, you begin to see things from God's perspective. He'll tell you amazing and wonderful things you may have never heard before—like you're more than a conqueror (Rom. 8:37) or you are a new creation (2 Cor. 5:17). Getting to know God's perspective and His character releases incredible power to change our perspective and our character.

This beautiful process of renewing our minds and becoming more like Him happens in countless small choices to recognize old patterns and choose new ones.

A New Identity

Before we met Christ, our identity was most likely shaped by our life experiences or by the people around us. But now that we are in Christ, we can see things more vividly and clearly, including who God truly created us to be. As a believer you have been given a new identity that transcends any previous identity you have ever had. Paul describes this astounding revelation that we experience when we truly understand who we are:

> God's Spirit touches our spirits and confirms who we really are. We know who he is, and we know who we are: Father and children. (Rom. 8:16–17 Message)

You have been adopted into God's family, completely forgiven and accepted—not because you've earned it, but because it's a free gift you've gladly received. You are not what you have done. You are not what "they" have said about you. And you are not what your past says about you. You are who God says you are! He knows every part of you because He formed you:

> You shaped me first inside, then out;
>   you formed me in my mother's womb.
> You know me inside and out,
>   you know every bone in my body;
> You know exactly how I was made, bit by bit,
>   how I was sculpted from nothing into something.
> (Ps. 139:13, 15–16 Message)

So then, who does God say you are? For starters, He says you are the righteousness of God through Christ Jesus. In your old identity, when you experienced failure, you may have felt stuck in the guilt and shame of that mistake. But this old identity is based on your own righteousness, not the righteousness of God. In your new identity in Christ, you could fail a million times and God would still love you and call you His own because He sees you only through the righteousness of His Son. Paul wrote about this incredible swap:

You are who God says you are!

> For He made Him who knew no sin to be sin for us, that we might become the righteousness of God in Him. (2 Cor. 5:21)

We are completely forgiven and totally accepted by God because Christ has imputed His righteousness to us and declared us to be righteous in His sight.

But your new identity doesn't stop at being called the righteousness of God. Ezekiel says that God gives us a new heart, Jeremiah informs us that we belong to God, Peter says that we're now part of a royal priesthood, and Paul proclaims that we have the privilege of being Christ's ambassadors. When we look in the mirror, we may look the same, but our passport has changed and our business card has a new title on it.

Today, choose to walk in your new identity in Him!

A New Sense of Confidence

As we become convinced about God's love and grace in the depths of our hearts, we gain a new, strong sense of confidence. My wife has always blown me away at her confidence in God and in herself. A couple of months after we had started Cornerstone Church, we lost our worship leader. As we talked about what to do next, she looked at me with eyes full of confidence and boldly declared, "I'll do it. I'll step up. I can lead." Her confidence in who God had called her to be both inspired and amazed me. The next Sunday she stood in front of the church and led worship for the first time in her life. I stood in the back of the church, mesmerized by her, and thought to myself, "My wife is kickin' powerful! I can preach my heart out after worship like that!" And that's exactly what we've been doing for over a decade since that day. Georgina now leads our main worship team every week, oversees four additional bands and worship teams as well as our performing arts department, and preaches at both our main campus and satellite campus. She's advancing His kingdom in a powerful way because she 100 percent believes that if God says she can do it, then she can do it!

If we are going to be revolutionaries who change the world for God, then we cannot be cowardly lions. We must be confident Christians! When a person speaks about the things of God with confidence, it's always a sign that God has brought wholeness to that person. They no longer see themselves as broken, fractured, or damaged. Today you can trust God with all the pieces of your heart, whether they are broken or intact, because His Word promises us that He will put all the pieces back together again.

> God made my life complete
>   when I placed all the pieces before him.
> When I cleaned up my act,
>   he gave me a fresh start. . . .
> I feel put back together. . . .
> God rewrote the text of my life
>   when I opened the book of my heart to his eyes.
> (2 Sam. 22:21–22, 25 Message)

The story of your life isn't over yet. Give God the pen of your heart today and watch as He begins to rewrite the story of your life! Today is your day for a fresh start!

12

Staying Open to Bigger Things

A person's world is only as big as their heart.
——Tanya A. Moore, author

Some lessons in life are learned by reading and some lessons are learned by having to live them out. Over the years I've maintained a conviction to stay open to bigger things. Prior to the church purchasing a nine-plex movie theater, there were two other facilities that I felt confident were going to be the home for our growing congregation. Both opportunities made complete sense, but the doors kept closing and God kept telling me, "Sergio, stay open to bigger things." I was discouraged because I felt that God had forgotten about me. But God was teaching me to stay open to bigger things. When we take the risk to follow Christ, God opens a whole world of possibilities to us—we become open to far bigger and better things than we ever imagined. Had

God given me what I wanted, we could never have facilitated the growth that we've experienced since then. Though God knows what you want, only He knows what you need! Now we are enjoying a facility that won first place in commercial interior design awarded by the American Society of Interior Design in all of San Diego County. It was the first time a church had ever won this prestigious award in National City. When I couldn't see what God was doing, I became tempted to settle, but He needed me to stay open for far greater things than I could ever imagine!

You may not be building a church, but you are building a family, a business, a career, a ministry. You are building a life that will glorify God. It's time for you to stay open to bigger things. Think about the opportunity to reconcile a relationship that has been out of reach. Think about the possibility of your friends and loved ones giving their hearts to Jesus Christ and experiencing this same Heart Revolution. Think about doors of financial opportunity opening to you that have been closed at your job. When you stay open to seeing these things come to fruition, you begin to believe that all things are possible!

Stay open to new relationships. Stay open to healing. Stay open to reconciliation. Stay open to the miraculous. Stay open to keeping all things in the realm of possibility. Like a loving father, God desires that His children come to Him and ask Him for anything:

> Ask and it will be given to you; seek and you will find; knock and the door will be opened to you. For everyone who asks receives; he who seeks finds; and to him who knocks, the door will be opened. (Matt. 7:7–8 NIV)

In a practical sense, staying open to bigger things simply means believing anything is possible. Your past may tell you only negativity and disappointments are in your future, but when you stay open to bigger things, there's no limit to what

God can bring into your life. I've seen countless men and women who have been single for years continue to stay open to getting married and end up meeting the spouse of their dreams when they least expected it. I've seen people who have lost their homes or businesses stay open to a second chance and receive that and more! I have seen too many people believe God for the unimaginable and receive it, for me to ever doubt that He has greater things in store for all those who will trust Him for more.

Kevin was married to Laura, his high school sweetheart, but slowly over the years they had become little more than strangers to each other. Life hadn't been easy for them as they experienced heartbreaking loss after loss. Gone were their hopes of owning a home after going through the pain of foreclosure. Gone were their aspirations of having a large family after two miscarriages. And gone were the dreams of a happy marriage after coming close to divorce on too many occasions. They lived in a state of mutual truce. At home, they avoided conversations because they always seemed to escalate into outbursts of anger and sarcasm. In an effort to keep peace in front of their daughter, they resolved to keep a reserved distance from each other, going through the motions of parenting as roommates instead of helpmates. Over and over, Kevin wondered, *What happened to us? How did we end up like this? Will things ever get better?*

Kevin was ashamed of the condition of his marriage but felt helpless to make it better. I remember preaching one Sunday about being open to God doing the unimaginable, when Kevin came up to me after service. Through pain-filled eyes, he pleaded for me to give him the answers. "Pastor, how can I get my life together?" I put my arm on his slumped shoulder and told him, "Just keep your heart open, Kevin. Keep coming with an open heart and God will turn things around. Take it one day at a time, but keep your heart open."

For the next three months, Kevin came to every service. As he sat in the same seat every week, God began to speak to him about opening up his heart to the possibility of restoring his marriage to what it once was. He began to trust that God wanted him and his wife to open up their lives and believe for more than just a common marriage. After every service, he'd go home and take the risk to open up the lines of communication with Laura again. He began to respond in truth to his wife, express words of love and appreciation, and pursue reconciliation at any opportunity

God wanted them to believe for more than just a common marriage.

he could. Laura began to see the sincerity of her husband, and the wall in her heart that had been built over the years began to crumble. She too began to open up her heart.

Over time they reestablished the covenant they had first made as husband and wife. They discovered a greater love for one another and a greater passion to parent their daughter. The change didn't happen overnight, but it came because Kevin and Laura decided to open up their hearts for more.

Many fractured families just like this have lost the hope that things can be different, but the good news is that God can redeem any broken relationship. When we are willing to trust Him for better things in our relationships, amazing things can happen. God is a big God and He wants us to live a big life! He wants us to know that He can do anything. When we feel tempted to doubt this, the words of the prophet Jeremiah remind us of His unlimited power:

> Dear God, my Master, you created earth and sky by your great power—by merely stretching out your arm! There is nothing you can't do. (Jer. 32:17 Message)

For many of us, before we opened our hearts to God, we had only one hand free to accept good things in life. We used the other one to hold our broken hearts. But now, both hands are free to accept His abundant blessings. As God acts for us and in us, marriages are restored, we learn to live above relational crises, and we trust God for greater things. We begin to live with a powerful blend of passion and peace.

Much of what we do at our church is the result of time I spend with God in prayer, asking Him to keep my heart open for greater things. Prayer is a part of my everyday life with God. For the last ten years, my mornings have begun in my backyard with my *One Year Bible*. Those times are sacred, because they open up my heart and mind to hear His direction and vision for my life and ministry. There have been mornings when I didn't want to pray and read, but there has never been a day when God did not speak into my life and encourage me to stay open for bigger things. These mornings have taught me the invaluable lesson that the larger my public life becomes, the greater my private life must become as well. In turn, I've discovered that much private prayer leads to much public power.

Jesus spoke openly about God's promise to hear and respond to our prayers when we come to Him:

> When you pray, go into your room, and when you have shut your door, pray to your Father who is in the secret place; and your Father who sees in secret will reward you openly. (Matt. 6:6–7)

If you will stay open to pray big prayers, God will do big things! As you grow in your personal obedience to God through this Heart Revolution, I encourage you to take the challenge found in the book of Malachi.

> "Test me in this," says the LORD Almighty, "and see if I will not throw open the floodgates of heaven and pour out so much blessing that you will not have room enough for it." (Mal. 3:10 NIV)

This is the only place in the Bible where God says, "Test me." We test Him by giving Him our best—our best financially, our best relationally, our best in every way. Giving Him our best allows us to walk in obedience and enjoy the blessings of greater things. Our obedience attracts the favor and blessing of God and sets an atmosphere in our lives where anything is possible.

Stay open to bigger things, because greater things are on their way!

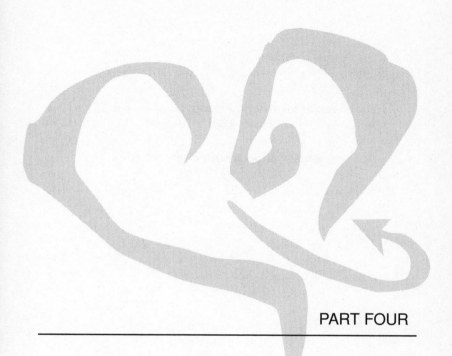

PART FOUR

THE "F" BOMB

Watch a special video message from Pastor Sergio
Part Four: The "F" Bomb

www.sergiodelamora.com/heartrev

13

The Forgiveness Factor

To forgive is to set a prisoner free and discover
that the prisoner was you.

—Lewis Smedes,
professor of ethics and theology

According to the Centers for Disease Control, the number one cause of death in America is heart disease. I've come to a similar conclusion about the vitality of a person's spiritual life. I have witnessed countless people experience spiritual heart disease due to unforgiveness. Their hearts have become clogged with the residue of hurts and offenses.

Forgiveness opens a pathway into our lives that allows the healing, peace, and favor of God to flow freely in and through us. Forgiving others is like breathing; you have to let out the bad air to make room for the good. When we hold on to unforgiveness, we run the danger of cutting off the source of our life. When we forgive, our hearts become uncluttered, allowing God to deposit the greatness of His call in our hearts.

Sadly, despite the benefits forgiveness offers, many people still struggle to let go of hurts, offenses, and grudges. Their struggle to forgive is oftentimes for one of two reasons—it's either too painful or they feel too powerless to forgive. But these emotions actually attract God to us.

> He gives power to the weak
> and strength to the powerless.
> Even youths will become weak and tired,
> and young men will fall in exhaustion.
> But those who trust in the LORD will find new
> strength. (Isa. 40:29–31 NLT)

Part of my job as a pastor is to help people have victory over their feelings of pain and powerlessness. The Moreno family was one decision away from healing. Many times Larry, a friend of the family, would stay with the Morenos while the two daughters and two sons were young. Unbeknownst to the parents, Hector and Norma, Larry took advantage of the two girls and sexually abused them for many years. Even more devastating was the fact that their brothers knew what was happening but had been threatened that if they ever told anyone, Larry would kill their parents. This pain was something these children wrestled with internally on their own for years. For them, forgiveness was unthinkable.

One family I met was one decision away from healing.

By the time the children were adolescents, the girls began acting out to cope with the hurt they had experienced. One of them reacted in rage at the slightest provocation. The other one became promiscuous, concluding that sex was the equivalent of being loved. The boys were also deeply affected.

One tried to mask the pain he felt for not protecting his sisters, while the other one drowned his anger in drugs and alcohol. All the children withdrew from Norma and Hector in their own way, unsure of how to cope with the abuse they had each endured.

After several years, the truth of what had happened came out, and the fragile threads holding the Moreno family together threatened to snap once and for all. Hector's immediate response was to pick up a gun and repay the sins that been done to his children. However, looking at the years of hurt and confusion in the faces of his kids, he decided to do the unthinkable. He chose to forgive.

He asked Larry to come over without his children present so that he could confront him with the truth. As these two men sat at the kitchen table with their faces inches apart, Hector asked for the truth. After what seemed like an eternity of silence, Larry broke down and wept in repentance. Hector was quiet, battling his own wave of emotions. Finally, he spoke. "You must ask my children for forgiveness."

Larry looked at Hector and Norma and sobbed as he begged for forgiveness from them. Although heartbroken, Hector looked into his eyes and told him, "I already have." Recognizing that these parents were pursing reconciliation rather than revenge humbled Larry even further. He went to each of the children and asked for forgiveness for the pain and abuse they had endured because of him.

Each one of their responses were different—anger, shame, denial, and fear. It took time, but eventually each of the children released both themselves and this man from the abuse, the offense, and the hurt for all they had endured. Through this process, the Moreno family talked about things they had avoided for years, and they became much closer than they had ever been. Hector had modeled forgiveness to such an incredible degree that the entire family experienced this miracle. Forgiveness had proven to be even more powerful than the hurt they had undergone.

Today, if there are any areas of unforgiveness in your life, let the love of Almighty God begin to heal the years of deep hurt that you've been carrying. As Psalm 34 tells us, He is right here, near the brokenness of your heart, ready to bring the healing that you need. He is your Healer and your Comfort. You can experience genuine forgiveness right now. Place your right hand over your heart and say these powerful words today:

Forgiveness is the greatest weapon we have as believers.

> *Father, as You forgave and released me from all that I have done, I release this situation and this person to You. I cancel the assignment this hurt has done or tried to do to me, in the name of Jesus. And I pray You would bring good things into my life, beginning now. I believe and receive that I can be free today.*
> *In Jesus' name. Amen.*

God loves you and forgives you without limit and without condition. As you become more and more convinced of His love and forgiveness, I pray that Paul's words will help you find the courage and strength to forgive those who have wronged you.

> Be gentle and ready to forgive; never hold grudges. Remember, the Lord forgave you, so you must forgive others. (Col. 3:13 TLB)

Forgiveness is the greatest weapon we have as believers. The Heart Revolution will challenge you and me to develop the ability to give and receive genuine forgiveness. This declares to the world that we are authentic in our walk with Christ. Our lives become open testimonies to the world that His message of reconciliation is real.

Forgiveness is the heart of the gospel and the foundation of every meaningful relationship. When we turn our hearts back to those we love, we begin to help them turn their hearts to God. Paul shares with us how the beauty of God's message of reconciliation was given to us so that we can in turn give it to the world:

> God has given us this task of reconciling people to him. For God was in Christ, reconciling the world to himself, no longer counting people's sins against them. And he gave us this wonderful message of reconciliation. So we are Christ's ambassadors; God is making his appeal through us. We speak for Christ when we plead, "Come back to God!" (2 Cor. 5:18–20 NLT)

The miracle of forgiveness brings healing not only in our life but also in the lives of those we forgive. It binds up the hurts that try to keep us stuck and broken and frees us from the prison of offense. Forgiveness accelerates the blessing of God in your life and unleashes the favor of God into your future.

When we choose to forgive, we are being more like Christ than at any other time in our lives. At that moment, when we drop the bomb of forgiveness, we detonate the presence of God in our lives. It's time to reach out to the person who hurt you. Don't wait. Your breakthrough is waiting for you to pick up the phone, send out the text, or write the letter.

14

The Courage to Ask
for Forgiveness

> The day the child realizes that all adults are imperfect, he becomes an adolescent; the day he forgives them, he becomes an adult; the day he forgives himself, he becomes wise.
>
> —Alden Nowlan,
> Canadian poet, novelist, and playwright

It's one thing when someone needs to ask us for forgiveness, but it's a different story when we are the ones who need to be forgiven. What hurts families, marriages, leaders, business partners, and friends most is the absence of courage to ask the questions that protect these relationships—questions such as, "Will you forgive me?" C. S. Lewis often saw through the mud of life to reveal the truth in the human heart. He observed, "Every one says forgiveness is a lovely idea, until they have something to forgive."

When we ask others to forgive us, we are choosing to become vulnerable to the point that we relinquish power to them. We are at their mercy and that takes tremendous courage. When we ask forgiveness from someone, we wrestle with feelings of weakness and inferiority. But doing so demonstrates the exact opposite. It reveals remarkable maturity, strength, and bravery.

Asking forgiveness reveals remarkable maturity, strength, and bravery.

One of the most courageous examples of this happened when two rival gang members started attending our church. Carlos and Tony, who on the streets were considered enemies, were now faced with the dilemma of having to view each other as brothers in Christ. They had known one another in prison and had fought many times before. Carlos had been a high-profile leader in the gang and was responsible for many of the crimes committed between the two gangs. Tony was the brother of a man who had been murdered by a member of the other gang. Because of their past history, they should have been throwing punches after taking one look at each other. But God had different plans for both these men.

They continued to come to Cornerstone and let God transform the image they had of both themselves and each other. They began to see each other as men, not enemies—but still not a word passed between the two of them. They would simply look at each other and look away. One Sunday I preached a message entitled "Breaking Out of the Prison Called Common," where I spoke about breaking out from the prison of the past. The Holy Spirit began to move in the heart of one of the men to finally break out from who he had been.

That day after service, Carlos, the man who had pledged loyalty to the gang that killed Tony's brother, approached Tony, looked him in the eyes, and asked for forgiveness.

Though Carlos had not been the one to pull the trigger, he extended his hand and asked Tony to forgive him for the loss and grief his family had suffered. No one knew exactly what would happen now that the first words had been spoken. Would Tony immediately respond in anger or violence? Could the history between them ever really be erased? Slowly Tony raised his hand to grasp Carlos's outstretched one. He spoke no words, but the handshake was enough.

The Justifier has the legal right to release us from the debt of sin.

Over the years, both these men left their former life for good and pursued a different mission. Instead of a life of violence, Carlos and Tony began to minister to thousands of young men and women about turning their hearts and experiencing genuine hope for a better life.

Think of when a person gives their life to Jesus Christ. To receive salvation, all God asks of us is that we come to Him and confess our need for Him. He offers us a new heart and a new life in exchange for our asking one simple question: "Lord, will You forgive me?" And here is God's response when we come before Him in a posture of humility, in need of forgiveness:

> If we confess our sins, He is faithful and just to forgive us our sins and to cleanse us from all unrighteousness. (1 John 1:9–10)

He is both faithful and just to forgive us. Faithful, meaning He will. Just, meaning He has the right to forgive. He is demonstrating His true nature to us as the Justifier with the legal right to release us from the debt of sin. He is saying to the world that, though we are sinners, justice has been satisfied. We no longer have to feel inadequate, because we have been forgiven by the One who determines justice. And all this is available to us when we ask the question, "Will You forgive me?"

One of the most beautiful illustrations of forgiveness is found in the story of a woman who took great risks for just a chance at forgiveness. Her steps must have been cautious as she entered into the room filled with those who despised her, but still she walked through. Ignoring the murmurings of disgust, she must have kept her head down and her eyes on the dirt floor until she reached Jesus, the one she had come to see. Now that she was just inches away from Him, shame and humiliation overtook her. She crumpled to her knees as tears began to stream down her face, and her heart wouldn't let her leave until she had done what she came to do:

> She brought an alabaster jar of perfume, and as she stood behind him at his feet weeping, she began to wet his feet with her tears. Then she wiped them with her hair, kissed them and poured perfume on them. (Luke 7:37–38 NIV)

This prostitute braved criticism, ridicule, and shame for the opportunity to sit at Jesus' feet and pour out her tears and oil. Though she never told Him the greatest desire of her heart, He knew. He loved her, protected her, and gave her the one thing no one else could give—forgiveness.

When we know that we've wronged someone by our actions or words, do we run to make it right? Are we quick to show our repentance for hurting someone? Do we take the stance of humility before the person we've offended? More often our first instinct is to rationalize why we chose to make the decisions we've made or marginalize the consequence of what we've done. We begin to make excuses to justify our actions. We tell ourselves, "They know I didn't mean it. They'll get over it. And if they don't, it's their problem." Not taking responsibility for our actions and asking for forgiveness leads to broken relationships, broken homes, and broken marriages.

If there are people you need to ask for forgiveness from, you can choose today to take the first step. You can choose to go to your parents, your in-laws, your children, your friends, and ask them one of the most powerful questions you've ever asked, "Will you forgive me?"

Asking for forgiveness releases the toxins of guilt, shame, and self-condemnation from your heart. Being honest about your mistakes lifts the burden off your shoulders and allows you to face each day without the fear of being confronted by people you've hurt. It's time for you to move on and look forward to new things instead of constantly looking over your shoulder, hoping that situation won't catch up to you.

Most importantly, when you seek forgiveness from others, you tap into God's heart and gain two valuable traits: humility and power. Humility is what brings His grace, His mercy, and His favor. Power brings the authority to live life with a sense of purpose and the confidence that you are not what you've done. It's the power that cancels the fear of punishment for your wrongs.

You can change the course of your relationships, beginning right now. You can move courageously in the direction of healing and restoration. Maybe you didn't make the phone call or send out the text yesterday. Maybe you didn't have the courage yet to hit "Send" on that email. Maybe it's a conversation that you've been putting off.

Today is your day. God will be there to help you with every step of the journey. He is just waiting for you to ask the question, "Will you forgive me?"

15

The Funk of Forgiveness

When you realize you've made a mistake, make
amends immediately. It's easier to eat crow while
it's still warm.

—Dan Heist, author

Too often, we think we've finished the process when
we ask for forgiveness. In most cases, though, that's
simply not enough. Countless believers wonder why
their spiritual lives stay lukewarm and their personal relationships remain strained and distant. Some of the problem is the
failure to complete the cycle of forgiveness. Yes, forgiveness
is free, but trust is earned.

In His most famous sermon, Jesus told the crowd on the
mountainside that day,

Therefore if you bring your gift to the altar, and there remember that your brother has something against you, leave

your gift there before the altar, and go your way. First be reconciled to your brother, and then come and offer your gift. (Matt. 5:23–24)

As we draw closer to God, He begins to speak to us about areas that we need to make right. We become aware of relationships that are still tender and in need of our attention. That's the picture Jesus paints in this passage. No matter where you are or what you're doing, when God reminds you that someone has something against you, He wants you to act immediately.

When God reminds you that someone has something against you, He wants you to act immediately.

Recently I did a study on the life of Joseph. As I read the story of Joseph's life, I became intrigued with his ability and willingness to forgive so quickly and easily. Despite the anguish and betrayal he had endured at the hands of his brothers, he was quick to open his arms to them and forgive every wrong that they had ever done to him. He didn't seek revenge or justice (Gen. 45:1–5).

He was in a position to punish them, but instead he chose to forgive and make amends. Why was Joseph so willing to forgive his brothers? How and when did he learn to be so forgiving? An obscure part of Scripture about Joseph's father, Jacob, reveals a powerful influence in Joseph's life.

Jacob looked up and there was Esau, coming with his four hundred men; so he divided the children among Leah, Rachel and the two maidservants. He put the maidservants and their children in front, Leah and her children next, and Rachel and Joseph in the rear. He himself went on ahead and bowed down to the ground seven times as he approached his brother. (Gen. 33:1–3 NIV)

Joseph watched his father bow before Esau to plead for forgiveness. He watched as his father offered gifts upon gifts in order to appease the heart of his brother. He watched every one of his father's wives, servants, and children bow before Esau in acknowledgment of the debt between the two men. And he watched these two men embrace and kiss one another in tears as brothers reconciled.

Joseph never forgot what he saw. Years later when he saw the same look of humility and repentance in the eyes of his own brothers, he followed the example of his father and wept as he embraced and kissed them.

Children first learn how to forgive and restore trust from their parents. The model we set today to refuse the temptation to hold grudges, harbor offenses, or seek revenge serves as a model for our children to constantly remind them of how to correctly handle conflict and disappointment.

> A good man leaves an inheritance to his children's children. (Prov. 13:22)

The greatest inheritance we as parents can leave for our children is the innate desire to make things right in our relationships. If you and I will sow a seed today of amendment, or change, in a relationship that is fractured or broken, we will reap a harvest, not only in our children, but also our grandchildren.

As a son, I've watched my own father model this same message of forgiveness, and as a result, today he is reaping a harvest of his inheritance in the lives of his children and grandchildren. I know that this is largely because he always chose to handle his relationships—with his wife, his children, his siblings, his business clients, his employees—with dignity, respect, and honor.

Over years of working with him, I've watched my father interact during hundreds, even thousands, of business transactions. And as in life, sometimes a project didn't go completely as planned. A mix-up occurred or a detail got missed, and the client looked to my father to see how he would handle the error. I've seen firsthand the humility of my father as he went back to fix every last detail of a project to preserve the integrity of a business relationship. And at home it was no different. These images are burned into my subconscious, and as I grew older they served as anchors to ground me in my relationships. As an adult when I needed to go back and mend a relationship, I would hear my father tell me, "Sergio, make it right. Do your part to make it right. God will take care of the rest."

"Do your part to make it right. God will take care of the rest."

Today, I want to tell you the same thing my father told me. Do your part to make it right, and let God do the rest. Maybe doing your part means paying back a financial debt to someone. Maybe it means restoring trust by reestablishing boundaries in a relationship. Maybe it means opening up the lines of communication after years of silence. Take the first step in making amends. Initiate. When you take steps to make your relationships right, go not only with an apology but also with the question, "What can I do to make it right?" A heart that longs to make amends will do whatever it takes to bring restitution.

This is what it means to be part of the Heart Revolution. We won't simply be satisfied to extend an apology and walk away. True reconciliation and forgiveness will pursue healing and restoration in every respect.

Jesus was the ultimate example of a person who made things right. Forgiveness is free because a payment was made in order to restore the relationship between God and us. God wanted to forgive, but a ransom was still required.

> According to the law of Moses, nearly everything was purified with blood. For without the shedding of blood, there is no forgiveness. (Heb. 9:22 NLT)

Jesus paid that ransom for us—for our children, for our grandchildren, and for all future generations—by His blood.

God longed for reconciliation to such a degree that He sent His Son to make amends on our behalf for sins we have not yet even committed. That is powerful!

As we enter into this forgiveness from God vertically, we see a transformation in our relationships horizontally. The more we come to the realization that God has already paid the price for our relationships to be made whole, the more we realize that we can, like Jesus, do whatever it takes to bring healing, reconciliation, and restoration into our lives.

Maybe you're thinking, "What if I go back and they don't receive me? What if they doubt the sincerity of my actions? What if it doesn't work out?" The beautiful thing about making amends is that you have time on your side. Keep doing the right thing. Keep moving toward restoration in small ways. Keep the lines of communication open. Don't get defensive or take a step back. Some people will receive you quickly; others may need more time to trust again. Over time, if you continue to keep rebuilding the bridge of trust, you'll win back that relationship.

Realize also that there are some who will reject your initial request only to hope that you will continue to pursue restoration. Trust time to soften what words could not in the hearts of those with whom you long to be reconciled. When you look for God's timing with your relationships, you free yourself from being tied to chronological time. Trust God's calendar, and as His Word promises, He will "make everything beautiful in its time" (Eccles. 3:11).

Today is your moment for restoration as you open up the doors of healing by choosing to make your relationships right. Your actions could very well restore not just a relationship but a life.

16

The Miracle of Forgiveness

He who is devoid of the power to forgive, is devoid
of the power to love.

—Martin Luther King Jr.

Forgiveness is often referred to as "the unnatural act."
One of the goals of the Heart Revolution is to overthrow this mindset. My prayer is that, as our hearts and
lives become revolutionized by Jesus Christ, we would begin
to instead see *un*forgiveness as "the unnatural act."

It's time for you and me to become professional forgiv-
ers who have mastered the art of forgiveness and releasing
offenses. Healthy relationships are not exempt from experiencing hurt. No, healthy relationships are those that have
learned the secret to letting go and moving on.

God is always thinking about your future, and there are key
moments when He will tell you, "It's time to move on." The

Israelites had a moment like this. When they were camped at Mount Sinai, God gave them the following order:

> You have stayed long enough at this mountain. Break camp and move on. (Deut. 1:6–7 GNT)

There comes a time when all of us must break camp and move on. Some of you need to break camp with the anger you've allowed to settle in your heart for another person. Some of you need to break camp with unforgiveness toward yourself—stop punishing yourself for a mistake you made many years ago. It's over.

Unforgiveness was never in God's plan for us. One of the most dangerous aspects of unforgiveness is that it keeps individuals and families bound to the lie that holding on to an offense for years and years somehow punishes the offender more than the offended. That is like drinking poison and hoping the other person dies. Too many families, too many homes, too many friends, and too many leaders have drunk from the poison of unforgiveness.

Healthy relationships are not exempt from experiencing hurt.

As you have journeyed through this book to this point, I believe God has spoken to you about areas that need His grace, His mercy, and His forgiveness. And as He has been faithful to cleanse those areas, the time has now come for you to draw a line that you will never cross again—the line against allowing unforgiveness to re-enter your heart. I encourage you to make this declaration:

> "I will not go back. I will not give room to unforgiveness, bitterness, and offense any longer. No matter what happens from this point on, I choose to move forward."

This is the true essence of the Heart Revolution.

One Sunday, Samantha, a girl in her twenties, heard me talking about revolutionizing relationships through forgiveness. She broke down after service, weeping over her relationship with her mom. For over twenty years, Samantha had watched her mother use heroin. Almost every day of her life she had watched her mom go into the bathroom for long periods of time and come out high. As a little girl, Samantha remembered throwing away needles, spoons, and bags of drugs in an effort to save her mother's life. She sobbed as she told me about the nights that she would cry herself to sleep, begging God to end one of their lives so that this roller coaster would finally stop.

> **"I will not give room to unforgiveness, bitterness, and offense any longer."**

Samantha had carried the ache of feeling abandoned, worthless, and rejected by the one person whose love she longed for. In all this pain, she developed her own addiction. Only hers wasn't with heroin like her mom. Samantha's drug was bitterness, anger, and unforgiveness. Through the tears, she shared how she had let anger and bitterness numb the pain of not having a mom to run to, to give her advice, to share her dreams with, and to cheer her on in life.

I looked at her intently. "After all the years of disappointment and resentment, Samantha, it's time to forgive your mom. Even if she's still using, forgive her. Not for her, but for you. Then God can bring you the miracle of forgiveness."

During the following months, Samantha began the process of letting go of memories and feelings that she had carried about her mom since she was a little girl. A line had been drawn in this young woman's heart that said, "No matter what happens, I'm not going back."

Samantha's mother struggled with heroin for two more years before finally turning her heart to God. Samantha wept with her mother at the altar as she repeatedly told her, "Mom, I forgive you." Years of guilt and shame fell from this mother's life as she cried with her daughter that day. It was the cry of healing, forgiveness, and restoration. Looking at these women today, you see no trace of who they once were. All you see is the miracle of forgiveness as this mom gets a second chance to make things right in the beautiful relationship she now has with her daughter and her grandchildren.

God wants to release the same miracle of forgiveness in your relationships. Samantha had every reason to remain hardhearted and bitter for the rest of her life, but she made the brave decision not to go back to the familiar emotions of her past. Just because she could didn't mean she should. She chose to move forward instead of staying stuck in her pain. She chose to pull out the roots of bitterness that had grown in the crevices of her heart. When she did, she revolutionized her heart and, in turn, her mother's heart and the hearts of her children.

Like the roots of a plant, the roots of bitterness and unforgiveness start slow, then begin to take over a person's heart until eventually growth becomes impossible. The writer of Hebrews warns us,

> Watch out that no poisonous root of bitterness grows up to trouble you, corrupting many. (Heb. 12:15 NLT)

No matter how much good seed is deposited, if the soil of a person's heart is hard, that seed will not grow.

Such offense even stopped what Jesus could do in His own hometown.

> "He's no better than we are," they said. "He's just a carpenter, Mary's boy, and a brother of James and Joseph, Judas and Simon. And his sisters live right here among us." And they were offended! . . . Because of their unbelief he couldn't do any mighty miracles among them except to place his hands on a few sick people and heal them. (Mark 6:2–3, 5 TLB)

No offense is worth hindering the miraculous from taking place in your life. No matter what has happened in the past, it's time to forgive. Your future depends on it. It's time to break camp with unforgiveness and move on. Draw the line in your heart and make a pledge never to go back to blame, pain, and shame.

People are waiting to be revived by your forgiveness. Your decision to forgive is powerful, not only in your life but in the lives of those you love.

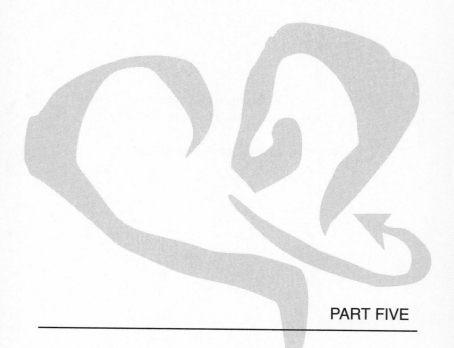

FINDING THE HEART
TO WIN AGAIN

Watch a special video message from Pastor Sergio
Part Five: Finding the Heart to Win Again

www.sergiodelamora.com/heartrev

17

Born to Win

When you say a situation or a person is hopeless,
you are slamming the door in the face of God.

> —Charles L. Allen, minister

We all love that moment in a movie when the underdog realizes he's not going to lose without a fight. With the roar of the crowd behind him and the taunting of defeat in his opponent's eyes, the unlikely winner musters up incredible strength from deep within to press through to victory. We cry and rejoice as though his triumph is our triumph as well. Inside every one of us is an inherent longing to win. It's called drive, momentum, and passion. And when we've lost it, we must take aggressive steps to find it again.

God wants you to start winning again—winning at home, winning with your children, winning at school, winning at work, winning wherever you go. There's a winner inside you!

I've heard it said, "Man can live about forty days without food, about three days without water, about eight minutes without air, but only for one second without hope." We all need assurance that even though life may look bleak at the moment, there is still the possibility that things will turn around for us. Sometimes all we need is just one touch of the living water to sprout again, like this word picture from the book of Job:

God wants you to start winning again!

> When a tree is chopped down,
> there is always the hope
> that it will sprout again.
> Its roots and stump may rot,
> but at the touch of water,
> fresh twigs shoot up. (14:7–9 CEV)

When you feel "chopped down" or you feel like your roots have become "rotted," sometimes all you need is one touch to renew your vigor. Just one touch of God's Word and your mentality begins to shift. Just one touch of His love and your heart begins to turn. Just one touch of His favor and your life begins to change. When you're at the end of your rope, you need one thing: a fresh sense of hope.

Hope isn't based on the expectation that everything will make sense or turn out exactly the way you want. Hope is much stronger than that. It is the conviction that God is with you, that He has a hidden purpose in everything you're experiencing. In your mind, the word *hope* may be only a wish or a dream. But in God's language, hope is the anchor that binds you to the everlasting truth that He is dependable, faithful, and trustworthy.

Over the years, I've come to the realization that most people desperately want to win but are afraid to believe again.

Our society is filled with thousands who just want to believe again. They've endured so much pain that they have become obsessed with fear. Men who have lost jobs or businesses have felt the sting of wounded pride and are now afraid to submit their applications again. Women who have endured the pain of losing a child are afraid to hope for another baby. Families who have lost their homes are afraid to believe they could ever own again. When you've been hit with losses such as these, it's hard to believe you can depend on God to give you victory. But read this declaration from David when the Lord saved him from Saul and his other enemies:

> The LORD is my rock, my fortress, my Savior.
> My God is my rock.
>   I can run to him for safety.
> He is my shield and my saving strength,
>   my defender and my place of safety.
>   The LORD saves me from those who want to
>   harm me. (2 Sam. 22:2–3 NCV)

This same God wants to be your rock when things get unsteady, your strength when you feel weak, and your refuge when you don't know where else to go.

Mario was a man who seemed born to lose. When he was eleven years old, his father taught Mario and his brother how to get high. A few years later, Mario's father went to prison and the boys were left to fend for themselves. From that moment, his life took a whirlwind journey downhill amid a myriad of drugs and alcohol. He married a woman who was an addict as well, but Mario was too fixed on the next time he could get high to see his life was taking one wrong turn after another. They had a daughter, but he barely spoke to her except to yell at her to get out of the room. Then things went from bad to worse. His daughter walked in one night to find her mother dead from a drug overdose. Mario was riddled with pain and guilt, and he had no clue how to help his daughter grieve. Father and daughter lived as strangers as Mario buried his head deeper into the ocean of denial and drugs. He married another addict who helped support his habit and raise his daughter. He waited for the day he would die so that the pain from all he had lost would finally come to an end.

Then the unexpected happened. He got a phone call from his father in prison asking for his forgiveness. Stunned, Mario listened as his father began to share with him that he had given his life to Christ in prison and now wanted to help his boys get off drugs. He wanted to make right the wrongs he had committed. Mario was speechless. He had no idea how to respond. He hung up the phone and immediately went to get high. But God had begun to orchestrate an opportunity for Mario to change his life. That phone call, along with an invitation to our church, brought Mario's wife through the doors of Cornerstone. She didn't understand what was happening to her, but she began to beg Mario to come with her. Within six months, they had both turned their heart and had begun to walk out sobriety. Their life did a complete 180. So much so that Mario's daughter wrote an essay in a contest for a brand-new pickup truck for her father. The line that leapt off the pages to the judges' hearts was when she shared that no one ever believed her father would change or have good things in his life. She wanted to give her dad a chance to feel like a winner, despite all that they had gone through. When Mario won that truck, no one could ever say that God had not turned his life around.

Maybe you know what it felt like for Mario to always lose, to always get knocked down in life. Just like Mario, you need to know you've got more in you. It's not over yet! You may be knocked down this round, but the final bell hasn't rung. You've still got one more round in you! Give your marriage one more round. Give your children one more round. Give your future one more round. Give God one more round. Decide to have a pit-bull faith that refuses to give up, sit down, or shut up. You've got one more kickin' round inside you!

Some of you may be thinking, "I want to give it one more round, but I don't know if I have the strength." All of us have felt so discouraged and exhausted that we've been tempted to throw in the towel. But if you will hold on, if you will stay in for one more round, you will find that victory is closer than you think.

Have a pit-bull faith that refuses to give up!

In the story of Gideon going to battle, he started with 32,000 men marching behind him but ended up with only three hundred. The text describes not only the condition of their bodies but the condition of their hearts as well:

> When Gideon came to the Jordan, he and the three hundred men who were with him crossed over, exhausted but still in pursuit. (Judges 8:4)

Though their bodies were tired, they refused to lose heart. They continued to stay in pursuit of their destiny. You have the right to be exhausted, but you don't have the right to give up your pursuit. When your body and mind threaten to give up, let the confident hope that victory is in sight propel you further. This is what made the difference in Gideon's leadership. He modeled to his 300 men that they weren't born to lose! They were born to win! And they did win. Those 300 men defeated over 15,000 warriors because they made a decision not to lose heart.

Gideon was not the only man in the Bible who faced the temptation to give up. In the New Testament, the people in Galatia were exhausted and on the verge of quitting. The Bible doesn't tell us exactly what troubles were wearing them down and chipping away at their faith. But think of what you go through today. Many of the same struggles we face today are similar to what the Galatians faced. But Paul assured them that they would see the fruit of their faithfulness when the time was right:

And let us not grow weary while doing good, for in due season we shall reap if we do not lose heart. (Gal. 6:9)

He was saying to them, "No matter what, don't quit!" God is telling you the same thing today: "Don't quit. Don't give up. No matter what, don't lose heart!" You weren't born to lose. You were born to win! Whatever you may be going through, this promise is for you:

He who is in you is greater than he who is in the world. (1 John 4:4)

The One on the inside of you—the greatest winner of all time, Jesus Christ—is in your corner, cheering you on as you find the heart to win again.

18

Recapturing the Real You

> Your inner speech, your thoughts, can cause you
> to be rich or poor, loved or unloved, happy or
> unhappy, attractive or unattractive, powerful or
> weak.
>
> —Ralph Charell, author

The number one crime in America is identify theft, and the number one crime in churches is spiritual identity theft. Too many people have been robbed of their identity in Christ and are now operating out of an identity that was never meant for them. Instead of being identified as a winner, they now associate themselves with the terms "loser" or "a disappointment." The reality is, they have become a victim of identity theft and they are now living out someone else's script for their lives.

Any film that has ever won a prestigious Academy Award has done so due largely in part to the scriptwriter. The scriptwriter sees the fullness of the characters before they ever take shape on the big screen. So it is with your heavenly Father and the script He has prepared for you in His Word—a script marked by victory and triumph. God Himself is the script-writer of your life!

As you begin to align yourself with His script and grow into the character He predestined for your life, you will discover that in His script you have all you need to win in life. Many times it can become easy to focus on the negative scripts people have written about your life. But when you do, you miss out on the power of living out a script marked with the greatness, purpose, and destiny contained in the one God has predestined for you.

In God's script you have all you need to win in life!

I know what it feels like to be scripted. While I was growing up, my parents had a script for my life that protected me when I found myself lost in another script of the neighborhood gang. My father had a dream that his children would take over his landscape design business and experience greater success than even he had seen. Both my parents saw my future in the family business, but I struggled to believe it was the right path for me. Yet even when I was trying to go my own way, they never once wavered or gave up on the script they had for me. They continued to believe in me and gave me room to assimilate the character God had shown them inside me. They could see greatness within me, but I struggled to see it. They had to trust that God's script would resonate louder than the script of my friends.

At seventeen, I didn't understand that going to work on the weekends with my dad was doing more for me than just teaching me the family business. I couldn't see the diligence, excellence, and responsibility being molded into me. All I knew was that every Saturday and every summer vacation I was going to be with my dad mowing lawns, digging ditches, and planting plants at some mansion in Santa Barbara. But now I can see how the ink from God's pen was constructing the storyline of my life. Every experience growing up would soon find its place in my destiny as an adult. I encourage you to trust the hand of Him whom you have trusted with your heart.

One day on the driveway of our home, I shared with my dad the news that my employment application was being considered at the city building department. I proudly explained that I would be making twelve dollars an hour instead of the six I was making with him. I was confident he would share in my pride and joy as I pursued a successful career just as he had done. Why would it matter if I was working for someone else? Surely he would just be proud of my decision not to settle for minimum wage. Success was important to him, so I eagerly awaited his approval.

My father sighed as he looked at me and said in Spanish, "Sergio, you're going to be making twelve dollars an hour working for another company when you could be making an unlimited amount working for yourself. This business is yours. Everything I do is for all of you. Don't you see you're already a millionaire?"

That statement infuriated me because I didn't feel like a millionaire. And when I read my bank statement, I knew I wasn't! But what my dad said next revolutionized my mentality about the acquisition of wealth. He said, "You're the boss here. What boss leaves his position to become someone else's worker? Think bigger, Sergio."

I was stunned at his words. In my father's script, I was the boss. In my script, I was the worker. His words changed everything for me that day. I refused the position with the city, took the pay cut, and never again questioned whether I was doing the right thing or making enough money. Over time my brothers and sisters came together in taking over my family's business, fulfilling my father's dream. Today, I'm proud to say that my father's script of success for his children is being carried out.

Perhaps the script written out for you wasn't one of success like the one my parents had for me. Perhaps it was the opposite. Maybe it was more like David's script, whose family and friends saw merely a shepherd boy instead of a warrior and king. David was ready when it came time for him to step into his character and fight Goliath, but not before he dealt with the script of his doubters and naysayers:

> "Don't worry about this Philistine," David told Saul. "I'll go fight him!" "Don't be ridiculous!" Saul replied. "There's no way you can fight this Philistine and possibly win! You're only a boy, and he's been a man of war since his youth." (1 Sam. 17:32–33 NLT)

David refused to change his script. He knew God had seen him through many battles before and he trusted the script that was written for him. He wouldn't give up on what he knew he could accomplish with God. But King Saul tried to rewrite David's script:

> Then Saul dressed David in his own tunic. He put a coat of armor on him and a bronze helmet on his head. David fastened on his sword over the tunic and tried walking around, because he was not used to them. "I cannot go in these," he said to Saul, "because I am not used to them." So he took them off. (1 Sam. 17:38–39 NIV)

David knew he couldn't find his victory in someone else's shoes, armor, or sword. He had to trust the winner God had put within him.

Your victory won't be found in the negative opinions or mentalities of others. You may have experienced defeat, but you are not defeated. God doesn't look at our past to determine our future. He looks at what He's predestined for our life and reminds us that our past is exactly that—the past. You can make a choice today to get up, brush yourself off, and press toward your goal. Let Paul's words become your own:

> I forget what is behind me. I push hard toward what is ahead of me. I move on toward the goal to win the prize. God has appointed me to win it. (Phil. 3:13–14 NIrV)

Let God begin to whisper to you His plans and purposes for your life. Let go of circumstances and thoughts that may have tried to define you. You were made to conquer. You were born to win. God knew from the beginning of time that you were set apart to do great things for Him. Just like He told Jeremiah, He is telling you today,

> Before I made you in your mother's womb, I chose you. Before you were born, I set you apart for a special work. (Jer. 1:5 NCV)

God chose you, set you apart, and predestined you to accomplish amazing things for Him. You weren't born by accident. You weren't a mistake. You are one of a kind, uniquely and wonderfully made, and every one of your days has already been prepared in advance (Ps. 139:15–16).

God doesn't look at our past to determine our future.

Let God's love and His script for you overshadow everything else you have heard, felt, or experienced. Let new words be imprinted across your heart—*redeemed, restored, renewed*—so that you can begin to live with a fresh sense of purpose and direction.

It's time to recapture the real you!

19

God's Strategy to Sustain Your Success

> By seeing the seed of failure in every success, we remain humble. By seeing the seed of success in every failure we remain hopeful.
>
> —Unknown

Every professional sports team in a championship game steps onto the field, court, or course with a strategy to win. From the moment the bell rings or clock starts, every player is focused on one thing—winning. Months of training have brought them to this moment, and they are prepared to give blood, sweat, and tears to finish in victory. They won't settle for second best. It's all or nothing, and those with the greatest tenacity and talent most often walk away the winner.

In the same way God wants you to walk in triumph and victory. In fact, Paul uses an athletic example to challenge the Corinthians to pursue a life of victory as well.

> You know that many runners enter a race, and only one of them wins the prize. So run to win! (1 Cor. 9:24 CEV)

God wants each and every one of us to live with the drive and motivation to succeed in every area of our life. Many times people have a misconstrued idea that God isn't interested in our success or victory, but the Bible says otherwise:

> And let them say continually,
> "Let the LORD be magnified,
> Who has pleasure in the prosperity of His servant."
> (Ps. 35:27)

The Bible clearly states that it pleases God to see you succeed. Every one of us has an instinctive quality that propels us further when the opportunity of victory is within sight. Over the years I've come across many people who have believed that their success isn't important to God. Somewhere in their lives they were led to believe that God **God wants you to walk in triumph and victory!** isn't interested in whether or not they have His best in their marriages, families, careers, education, and spiritual lives.

However, Scripture tells us that God uses our testimonies in these areas as examples to the rest of the world. How else can He compel the world to know His faithfulness, goodness, and mercy unless our lives bear witness? God loves to see His children win in every area, because through our success, He is glorified. When our marriages win, He gets the glory. When our kids win, He gets the glory. When our families win, He gets the glory. When we win, He wins because our lives become examples of His restoring power, His immeasurable goodness, and His undeniable favor. We are His trophies to the world:

But thanks be to God, Who in Christ always leads us in triumph [as trophies of Christ's victory] and through us spreads and makes evident the fragrance of the knowledge of God everywhere. (2 Cor. 2:14 AMP)

For two years I coached my daughters' soccer team and was told by some, in their effort to protect the girls from disappointment and failure, not to encourage them to focus on winning. The mentality was to just help them do their best so they would simply feel the satisfaction of playing. But to play without a goal, drive, or motivation wasn't helping them "do their best." It was in actuality doing a great injustice to them.

Through our success, God is glorified.

Their potential was not going to develop without the opportunity to experience victory. They wanted to strive for more. They wanted to press through to win. They wanted to play with a sense that they were giving all they had on the field at every game and at every practice. They yearned to feel the rush of accomplishment.

When the girls won, they wanted to practice harder to win again. And when they lost, they wanted to do anything they could to get better. Every one of the girls wanted to walk away and say they had won some games, won some new friends, and most importantly won their self-respect. At the end of the season they had pushed themselves farther than they thought they could and as a result had redefined their understanding of "doing their best."

I think back to those days and wonder what would have happened if we had just let those girls play with direction but no motivation. Would they ever have known what they were capable of without stretching their limits to reach toward the goal of winning? They broke through limitations and expectations by choosing to pursue victory instead of mediocrity.

I've counseled countless people who have chosen to downsize or marginalize their dream because they didn't want to risk failure. I've met just as many people who are equally afraid of success. They veer away from pursuing success because they don't want to face the pressure, expectations, and pace that are associated with a successful life. The reality of having to maintain their success becomes the reason they would rather settle for mediocrity. They would rather settle for second best than live with the weight and pressure of having to sustain success.

"Lord, keep me blessed, keep me broken, and keep me obedient."

You were never meant to live a second-best life. You were meant to live out God's best. Success doesn't have to be a scary word, because God's version of success doesn't come with the world's expectations and pressures. God's success is built on the premise that you're already a winner, so why not live it out? He has already given you the tools and resources to live with a first-place mentality. Why not just believe you can have a first-place marriage, a first-place family, a first-place career, and first-place kids?

Even if you've felt the sting of disappointment or failure in the past, God's love will carry you toward victory:

> But in all these troubles we have complete victory through God, who has shown His love for us. Yes, I am sure that nothing can separate us from God's love—not death, life, angels, or ruling spirits. I am sure that nothing now, nothing in the future, no powers, nothing above us or nothing below us—nothing in the whole created world—will ever be able to separate us from the love God has shown us in Christ Jesus our Lord. (Rom. 8:37–39 ESV)

Through my journey as a Christian and a pastor, I have felt the pain of disappointment and the sting of defeat, but out of these moments has come one of the most powerful prayers I have ever prayed: "Lord, keep me blessed, keep me broken, and keep me obedient." Jesus fed the multitudes with a few loaves and fish by this same principle (Mark 6:39–44). He blessed it and broke it, and it fed thousands. In the same way God wants to keep us blessed so that we will live with a sense of significance for His kingdom, broken so that we are in constant need of Him, and obedient so that we never deviate from His plan for our life. I'm telling you again that you can win and keep winning if you will keep this principle in motion.

Even when you feel as though the finish line is out of your reach, be confident that God will complete the good work He began in you (Phil. 1:6). His strategy for you was designed not for you to win once, but for you to *keep* winning in every area of your life!

20

Propelled by Purpose

You were made by God and for God, and until you
understand that, life will never make sense.

—Rick Warren

In the world of business, entertainment, politics, sports,
finance, and practically every other aspect of life, power
is king. In these arenas, people strive to get to the top so
they can control their own purpose and destiny. They would
rather be the one in control than the one who is controlled.
But the Heart Revolution is not about getting to the top
and determining your own destiny. It's about becoming empowered to live out the purposes and destiny that God has
predestined for your life! Now that your heart is turned, your
life is now turned to God's direction and purposes. Instead of
building up someone else's kingdom, you're building God's
kingdom. You are His beloved, a co-heir with Christ, and

His ambassador who represents Him to everyone you meet. What propels Him, now propels you. You were created *on* purpose and *for* a purpose.

So the question now becomes, What is God's purpose for your life? As a pastor, this is the question I get asked most. God's purpose for each and every one of us is the same—to know Him and make Him known. How we do that lies in our unique and individual callings. The highest purpose we could have is to know God and reflect His glory and goodness to our families, to our neighbors, and to people around the world. This is why when Jesus healed a demon-possessed man, He told him to go back to his family instead of allowing him to go with Him:

God's purpose for each one of us is the same—to know Him and make Him known.

> As Jesus was getting into the boat, the man who had been demon possessed begged to go with him. But Jesus said, "No, go home to your family, and tell them everything the Lord has done for you and how merciful he has been." (Mark 5:18–19 NLT)

The greatest use this man could be to the kingdom was to tell as many people as he could what Jesus had done to revolutionize his life. We have the same mandate today. As our hearts get revolutionized, our purpose becomes more clear. You become a turner of hearts, because the One who's on the inside of you has turned yours.

To most people the Heart Revolution is simply a church idea. But to you and the thousands of others who have experienced the love, forgiveness, and power of Christ, this revolution is real. You are the greatest billboard for God to those around you. You have been healed to bring others to the Healer. You have been restored so that you can introduce others to the Restorer. And you have been revolutionized by Him to become a revolutionary.

One of the most rewarding aspects of being a pastor is the opportunity God has given me to speak into the hearts and lives of young people. It's a privilege to be able to pastor the next generation and watch God develop their potential.

Felipe was a young man whose story I will never forget. Felipe had grown up in a family that had modeled to their children the importance of prayer, reading the Bible, and having faith in God. They were leaders in their church, faithfully serving for over ten years, until one day everything changed. Their pastor had made painful decisions that scarred his testimony and crushed the church until eventually it shut down. Felipe's parents were devastated. They let go of everything and walked away from their faith. Though they never got connected to another church, they didn't stop Felipe from coming to church when a classmate invited him.

You have been revolutionized to become a revolutionary!

One day, Felipe told me, "Pastor, my family doesn't understand all the time why I still choose to follow God after all we've been through. But the most powerful thing I have is my testimony. I want to make a difference. If I lose my testimony, I lose the one thing that I've worked so hard to build. Even though they don't understand, I gotta keep coming. I'm not giving up until my family comes back to church." His intuitive words were remarkable.

Not long after that conversation, Felipe found out that his mom had been diagnosed with stage three cancer. I expected him to show up at the next service with tears in his eyes, but he didn't. He saw me across the parking lot, smiled at me, and went into the sanctuary to help set up chairs just as he had done for the past year. During that service, all of our youth watched as Felipe lifted his hands and voice to God in worship. Not once during that night did he lose his smile.

That night after service I went up to him and asked him how he was doing. He smiled at me again and said, "Pastor,

I'm great. The doctor says my mom has cancer, but I'm calling it her miracle. I'm praying this is what brings her back to church. Maybe that's the whole purpose behind this. I know God can do anything. So instead of thinking she has cancer, I just see it like she's got a miracle on the inside of her that God's going to use to show the world how big He is. Pretty cool, huh?"

I smiled back at him and said quietly, "Yeah. Pretty cool."

I walked away with tears in my eyes at Felipe's faith. When his mom started chemotherapy, Felipe was there holding her small, feeble hand to pray. When she went into surgery to remove the tumors, Felipe was there on his knees crying out to God for his miracle. Through the next five years, Felipe stood by his mom and never wavered in his faith for her. He would come every week to church with that same angelic smile, believing for a miracle he knew would come. He believed his purpose was to have enough faith not only to get through this, but for his mom to get through it as well. After five long years of fighting, Felipe's mom lost her battle to cancer and passed away.

I held him in my arms as he cried at the end of a journey that had changed him in every way except one—his faith. He looked at me and asked me to officiate his mother's funeral. His one request was for me to do an altar call at the end of the service. "Pastor, there has to be a bigger purpose in all of this. I don't want this to be another reason for the rest of my family to go farther away from God. Help me bring them back."

Three nights later, after a tear-wrenching eulogy from Felipe, I humbly walked onstage. I stared out into the sea of faces and asked if there was anyone there that needed to get right with God. Felipe's father put his arm around his son and slowly raised his hand to rededicate his life to Christ. One by one, more and more hands began to rise throughout the room. I choked back tears as I led hundreds of Felipe's friends and family through the prayer of salvation. When he saw the overwhelming response, he looked at me, still locked in his father's embrace, and smiled. Then he looked around at all the raised hands and mouthed two words that sent a chill down my body: "My miracle."

This teenager, this revolutionary, had renamed his rival. Instead of calling it cancer, he called it his miracle, and as a result, he had the greatest victory he had ever experienced.

I believe there are cancers in our life today that God wants us to rename. There's a miracle in that situation if you will just believe like Felipe did. Your purpose is being revealed through that situation. God will turn that mess into your ministry and that test into your testimony. Let every day of your life be infused with His purpose to show the world how big He is.

You are a miracle, and every day is your opportunity to show the world He is real!

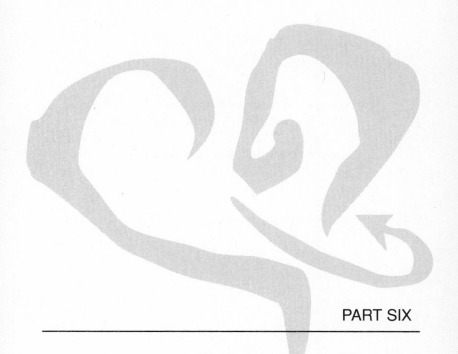

KEEPING YOUR
HEART HEALTHY

Watch a special video message from Pastor Sergio
Part Six: Keeping Your Heart Healthy

www.sergiodelamora.com/heartrev

21

A Willing Heart

The good and the great are only separated by the willingness to sacrifice.

—Kareem Abdul-Jabbar, basketball legend

The first twenty days of *The Heart Revolution* focused on you and your relationship with God. We've talked about how God uses your pain to awaken your need for Him, and you've seen how God wants you to trust Him, follow Him, and believe in His plan. Now we turn a corner. The next twenty days address the overflow of God's love from your heart to the lives of those around you. Because you've genuinely experienced the love of God, He reminds you of where you've been, without condemnation or guilt, so that you can bring the Heart Revolution to other people.

When we use the word "heart," we naturally think of both the physical and the spiritual heart. The parallels are important. The heart that beats in our bodies is located near the center of our chests and controls the lifeblood that flows in and out. In the same way, a spiritual heart that seeks God puts Him in the center of our thoughts, desires, and purposes. Our physical heart is about the size of a clenched fist. Our spiritual heart, on the other hand, grows as large and strong as we desire. There is no limit to how great our spiritual hearts can become.

God chose David based on the quality of his heart.

David was one of the greatest leaders the world has ever known. But David also knew what it was like to live on both the right and wrong track with God. When God chose him from among his brothers to be the next king, it was based on the quality of his heart. The Bible says God told Samuel,

> Do not look at his appearance or at his physical stature, because I have refused him. For the LORD does not see as man sees; for man looks at the outward appearance, but the LORD looks at the heart. (1 Sam. 16:7)

David may not have looked like the one most likely to succeed, but that didn't matter to God. He saw what was in his heart.

One of the most important heart qualities that positions us to be greatly used of God is that of willingness. A willing heart says to God, "I will go where You send me and I will do what You ask of me." When He knows that He can rely on us to say yes to Him, His favor flows to us and allows us to be used for His glory. God can use us to turn the hearts of others when the condition of our hearts is willing, like the response of Jonathan's armorbearer when he was asked to engage in war against thousands with only himself and Jonathan. It seemed like a suicide mission but he responded with a willing heart to do whatever was asked of him:

> So his armorbearer said to him, "Do all that is in your heart. . . . Go then; here I am with you, according to your heart." (1 Sam. 14:7)

His armorbearer didn't give excuses when he was asked to step out. He didn't complain or give arguments. He was willing to go wherever he was needed. Today God is looking for the same willing heart in us. He is looking to see if we will be willing to do all that is in His heart for us, instead of giving Him our excuses or arguments when He asks us to step out for Him.

Jesus told the parable of a man who held a great supper and invited many. But in response to his invitation, all he got back was excuses. Some used the excuse of family and marriage. Some used the excuse of being too busy taking care of their land or home. And others used the excuse of their jobs (Luke 14:16–24). Today, we may be tempted to give God similar excuses. But a willing heart steps out for Him, even when it's inconvenient.

When I think of a willing heart, I think of my wife, Georgina, and my daughters. When we came to San Diego, Georgina didn't just pack up her life and move to a new community, a new city, and a new home. She packed up the lives of our three small children as well, all while being seven months pregnant. She enrolled them in new schools, helped them say goodbye to friends and family, and prepared a home for them in a city where they knew no one. Never once did they complain. Never once did they argue. Never once did they make excuses. All they said was yes.

Even as Georgina said goodbye to her mom, whom she sat and had coffee with every morning, she never complained. And even as my daughters left behind best friends and cousins, they never complained. They never gave God a reason to disqualify them from being used by Him. At that pivotal moment in their lives, the only characteristic He was looking for wasn't talent, intellect, gifting, or skill. He was looking for willingness of heart.

The willingness Georgina and our daughters displayed personifies what God is looking for in those whom He greatly uses. So many people want to arrive but don't want to take the trip. When we focus on the challenges or hardships that come from obeying God instead of focusing on the journey, we may miss a life-changing moment with God. Take for example this illustration. Imagine an all-expense-paid thousand-mile road trip offered to two families—only the destination is a secret. One family complains about the long drive and all the negative things that might happen and decides not to accept; another family looks at the trip as an adventure and agrees to it. How glad will the second family be that they were willing to go when they see the first signs that point to their destination—Disney World? The journey with God will always lead to a destination that is far better than we could ever have dreamed.

In the Bible, Abraham was given this same test. God told him all the wonderful plans He had in store for him, but it required that he have a willing heart.

> The LORD had said to Abram, "Leave your native country, your relatives, and your father's family, and go to the land that I will show you. I will make you into a great nation. I will bless you and make you famous, and you will be a blessing to others. I will bless those who bless you and curse those who treat you with contempt. All the families on earth will be blessed through you." So Abram departed as the LORD had instructed. (Gen. 12:1–4 NLT)

What I love about the story of Abraham is that this conversation happened when he was seventy-five years old! Abraham could have very easily given God the excuses of being too old, too settled, too comfortable to go out to a place that wasn't even disclosed to him. But the Bible says Abraham did as he was instructed. As a result of that one heart decision to be willing to go wherever God sent him, Abraham is known and accredited as the father of many nations. In fact, the book of Matthew records the lineage of Jesus beginning with Abraham. When you say yes to God, you have no idea how many amazing blessings are on the other side of your obedience!

I believe there are things that God has been speaking to you about even as you have journeyed through this book. Say yes today to God's plan for your life and say yes to a greater future than you could ever have imagined! All it takes is a willing heart.

Keep your heart open and healthy before God.

Your heart is everything. It is the great qualifier that either causes you to advance in your purpose or to sit out for a season. Take for example the story of Caleb. You don't hear much about Caleb, but what you do hear reveals the willingness of his heart. When it was his moment to lead the children of Israel into the Promised Land, he took it. And as a result, Caleb had the privilege of stepping into his purpose and destiny.

> [The Lord said,] "But My servant Caleb, because he has a different spirit in him and has followed Me fully, I will bring into the land where he went, and his descendants shall inherit it." (Num. 14:24)

Caleb is a classic example of someone who had lived in obscurity, but the quality of his heart launched him into his purpose at the right moment. I call that a Caleb moment—a defining moment when God shows us a glimpse of what our future can look like. Never underestimate your moments in obscurity. God has sent Caleb moments into your life to propel you further into your purpose and destiny. Your assignment as a revolutionary is to keep an open heart before God so that when your Caleb moments happen, you'll be ready!

In the days of ancient Israel and Judah, the prophet Hanani told King Asa,

> For the eyes of the LORD run to and fro throughout the whole earth, to show Himself strong on behalf of those whose heart is loyal to Him. (2 Chron. 16:9)

Today, God's eyes still run to and fro, looking for people whose hearts are willing. He wants to use you to bring His plans and purposes to life. Whether you've been serving God for thirty years or thirty days, keep qualifying your heart before Him. All it takes is the decision to turn your heart to Him daily. No decision will ever be as rewarding, as empowering, or as revolutionary.

22

Converting Adversity
from Foe to Friend

> For many people, it takes the jolt of tragedy, ill-
> ness, or death to create an existential crisis of
> faith. At such a moment, we want clarity; God
> wants our trust.
>
> —Philip Yancey

Over the years I've been asked, as a pastor, how I keep
my passion for God. My answer is "adversity"—the
tension of encouragement and affliction that has kept
me in constant need for more of God.

Our natural reaction is to run from adversity, and when
we can't avoid it, we do everything we can to minimize the
pain. But what if we look at adversity as God sees it—the
raw material of great faith?

Many people view adversity as a sign you're on the wrong track, but that may not be God's viewpoint. Many times adversity is one of the greatest signs that you're on the *right* track. Your first reaction may be to defend yourself or to run from it. That's entirely normal.

Adversity is the raw material of great faith.

But before you react, understand that every opposition can be a stepping-stone for your faith. Sometimes, adversity is really God testing you so you'll learn to trust Him more. I want to encourage you to view opposition and testing in a new way. Begin to see adversity as a tool in the hand of God to focus your mind and heart like nothing else can. See adversity through God's eyes—allow it to be your gateway to greatness.

When I was in the landscaping business, getting cuts and bruises was part of the territory. I remember my dad sending me to clear out old rosebushes for a new rose garden. Those old bushes were covered with some of the worst thorns I'd ever seen. Each time an inch-long thorn pierced through my gloves, pain shot through my body, and I became instantly and completely focused on the point of the pain. It's the same in the emotional and relational realm. When you experience conflict, heartache, and disappointments, you no longer keep rolling along without a moment of reflection. You're forced to stop. You want to know what happened, why it happened, and how to stop it from happening again.

But here's the difference between God's perspective and our perspective of adversity. He is challenging you to no longer see adversity as something happening *to* you, but instead to take on the perspective of it happening *for* you. God will always use adversity to focus your thoughts and attention on Him so that you can see His hand and hear His voice more clearly.

As you continue to live out the Heart Revolution, there may be times when the enemy lines up a full array of attacks to knock you out of the battle. He may use deception, discouragement, accusation, or even a combination of all three. He'll try to put roadblocks in your way to slow you down so that you'll quit. He'll accuse you of being inadequate and unqualified to serve God. Don't fall for the enemy's tactics. Be on guard to protect your heart and fight hard against his schemes. Paul was wise to the enemy's devices. Can you see him pacing like a general commanding his troops when he dictated these words?

> Put on the whole armor of God, that you may be able to stand against the wiles of the devil. For we do not wrestle against flesh and blood, but against principalities, against powers, against the rulers of the darkness of this age, against spiritual hosts of wickedness in the heavenly places. Therefore take up the whole armor of God, that you may be able to withstand in the evil day, and having done all, to stand. (Eph. 6:11–13)

In times of adversity, we aren't alone. We have God's power and guidance, and we have the wisdom and experience of others who are in the fight and have endured the same kind of attacks. When God told me to start a Heart Revolution, I had no idea the magnitude and impact it would make in the lives of so many people. I just knew what He had told me to do. But out of this revolution have come some of the most powerful testimonies of faith, victory, and triumph I've ever known. And it all started with a decision to turn their hearts.

God uses adversity to focus your thoughts and attention on Him.

Ryan had come from a good family. With both parents in executive positions and making six-figure salaries, Ryan had wealth, prominence, and potential. But he also had a secret. He had secretly struggled with depression since his teen years. By the time he hit his twenties, he was desperate for a change. He longed to come out from beneath the dark clouds that seemed to follow him everywhere, as constant thoughts of negativity and suicide bombarded his mind. When adversity came, Ryan fought the urge to run and hide. He had a decent job and seemed like just a quiet guy to coworkers, but no one knew that every night Ryan would go home to a dark, empty apartment where he'd sit for hours on end, alone in his thoughts. With no one to turn to, Ryan was like a time bomb just waiting to self-destruct.

A coworker invited him to a Bring a Friend service, and initially he refused. But she persisted for weeks. Eventually, he agreed to come. At the end of that service, I asked if there was anyone that needed a fresh start. Immediately his hand shot up. For the first time in his life, Ryan felt a glimmer of hope. Grabbing onto God with everything he had, he quickly joined a life group, became involved in our covenant classes, and began his journey out from under depression.

Some weeks were better than others, and some were worse. But he kept showing up. When Ryan lost his job due to pay cuts, instead of running, he kept coming to church. And when he lost his car, instead of giving up, he took the bus and still kept coming to church. Nothing stopped him from showing up every week. His reason? He said, "Every time I show up and do the opposite of what I used to do, I win. Every time I do what I used to do, depression wins. And I won't let that happen anymore. The day I turned my heart, I made a decision to stop losing." This is how Ryan converted adversity from foe to friend—he just kept showing up.

Those who have endured struggle and hardships in the past know they aren't immune from it happening again. But like Ryan, in Christ, adversity becomes the building blocks of faith, perseverance, and victory. All of us will experience adversity at some point and in some way—it's an essential ingredient in God's plan for us. When it happens, we can make heart decisions to stop losing too. Make these decisions today and start converting adversity from foe to friend:

- Make a heart commitment to *grow from*, not just *go through*, adversity.
- Make a heart commitment to trust God to use pain to *purify* you, not *penalize* you.
- Make a heart commitment to *humble* yourself before God instead of *defending* yourself.
- Make a heart commitment to *wait patiently* for God's answers and directions instead of *reacting* out of raw emotions.

You may be in the middle of adversity today. If you are, make a heart commitment to trust God to give you the wisdom, strength, and courage to accept adversity instead of running from it. When I reflect back on the greatest seasons of growth in my life and in our church, it never ceases to amaze me that these moments were almost always preceded by the greatest seasons of adversity. It's almost as if adversity is an announcement from heaven that promotion is on its way!

Think about the times of adversity in your life. Isn't it true that your marriage became stronger as a result of adversity? Isn't it true that the relationships that endured adversity are the ones you cherish the most?

Adversity isn't your enemy. It's your friend. As long as you remember that, you'll never lose the battle of adversity again.

23

Habits of the Heart

> Motivation is what gets you started. Habit is what
> keeps you going.
>
> —Jim Rohn, motivational speaker and author

The disciples in the early church were making waves by
doing uncommon things, like healing the sick and leading thousands to Christ. In an effort to suppress their
influence, religious leaders arrested them and put them in "a
common prison" (Acts 5:12–18). I believe today in the heart of
every person there is still a struggle against this prison called
"common." Too many people are being held there, either by
their own perspective or because of the labels others have
placed on them. But just like the disciples, you are not average.
You aren't ordinary. And you're far from common.

Your habits, often called spiritual disciplines, are the key
to living out this uncommon life of a revolutionary. When

you've come from a life of addiction and have seen what negative habits can do to a person, you realize that unless you develop new habits, you might end up in the place you were before. When I became a Christian, I knew that unless I changed my habits I wasn't going to make it. I began to pray a simple prayer that helped me create new habits of the heart: *Lord, give me a hunger and desire for You and Your Word.* I am still feeling the ripple effect of this prayer today.

That prayer launched me into a passion for reading His Word in any form I could get into my hands. I would buy and borrow books to keep my heart saturated in His Word. I traded my habit of collecting records and memorizing beats for collecting biblical commentaries and memorizing Scripture. Instead of staying up late to party, I was now staying up late to study Greek and Hebrew. To the amazement of my family, I filled my room with books to read instead of records to play. The ironic part of this new habit was that, in elementary school, reading was not my strongest subject, to say the least. I developed a passion for reading and studying that today has served me well. Through those early days, I learned that developing healthy heart habits, as part of a lifestyle, is vital to maintaining your passion and fire to live, lead, and love from the heart.

The disciplined man always wins.

In *The Disciplined Life*, Richard Taylor states, "The disciplined man always wins." In every area of life—business, academics, parenting, and pastoring—a little edge can tip the scales in your favor. It's personal disciplines that give you the edge that make the difference, not necessarily between winning and losing, but between being sharp and being dull, being effective and being mediocre. Where does the motivation come from to push a little harder? From having a clear view of the finish line.

We have to know what we're trying to accomplish before we start. Your personal finish line may be seeing your entire family come to Christ, or having your heart renewed with a stronger passion to lead, or developing your potential as a person, partner, and parent. Whatever your finish line is, you need healthy habits of the heart to get you there. Let's look at habits that give you the edge to living a revolutionary life.

Daily Bible Reading

Reading our Bible every day is a habit we, as revolutionaries, must develop. The Bible is God's Word for you every day and spending time in His Word gives you the necessary tools needed to know His direction for every situation. For the past five years, our church has collectively read the *One Year Bible* together. God has consistently spoken to us as individuals and as a church body through our readings. This reading plan includes a portion of the Old and New Testaments, as well as Psalms and Proverbs.

Maybe you've tried to read the Bible before and you gave up because you struggled to understand it. Today, I encourage you to try again. Pick up a *One Year Bible* and begin your own comprehensive reading plan of the Bible. Reading the Word of God daily will bring His power, His truth, and His revelation into your everyday life.

> For the Word of God is alive and powerful. It is sharper than the sharpest two-edged sword, cutting between soul and spirit, between joint and marrow. It exposes our innermost thoughts and desires. (Heb. 4:12 NLT)

There is a difference between reading the Bible and letting the Bible read you. Start reading your Bible every day and begin to see the living power of His Word become active in your life. The Bible isn't just a book. It's alive, penetrating every area of your life so that God's thoughts become your thoughts and His desires become your desires.

Daily Prayer

Connecting with God is no different than connecting with anyone else. Prayer is your direct line to God. And spending time in prayer isn't only about talking to God. It's also about listening. As you pray, take time to be quiet and listen. There's a temptation to fall into the dull practice of making prayer just a list of the things you need from Him. In one of His teachings to the disciples, Jesus gave them the template on how to pray:

In this manner, therefore, pray:

> Our Father in heaven,
> Hallowed be Your name.
> Your kingdom come.
> Your will be done
> On earth as it is in heaven.
> Give us this day our daily bread.
> And forgive us our debts,
> As we forgive our debtors.
> And do not lead us into temptation,
> But deliver us from the evil one.
> For Yours is the kingdom and the power and the
> glory forever. Amen. (Matt. 6:9–13)

When you pray, begin by remembering that He is not a distant, uninterested God. He is your Father in heaven. Then tell God how amazing, magnificent, and holy His name is. Next, start asking for His will and His kingdom to be established in your life. Then ask for His provision, forgiveness, and protection. Finally, declare His dominion and power, which places His seal of authority on your words.

Your prayers are powerful! Don't make it a once-in-a-while event. God has a lot to say to us every day. We just need to listen.

Confession

Confession before God isn't about reciting a list of things you've done wrong. It is an invitation for genuine relationship with Him rather than simply penance. To *confess* literally means "to agree with." Through a daily honest confession, you agree that you've made mistakes, you agree that Christ has forgiven you, and you agree that you need to make better choices next time. It's a partnership with God, inviting Him to daily examine your heart, and then responding in faith to whatever He shows you. God already knows when you've taken a wrong step away from His plan. He just wants to know if you'll come to Him and accept His forgiveness.

Even more powerful is the fact that you're not alone in your confession. The Bible tells us that it's Jesus who acts on your behalf, mediating, interceding, and reconciling you back to God:

> For there is only one God and one Mediator who can reconcile God and humanity—the man Christ Jesus. (1 Tim. 2:5 NLT)

Learning to confess is an important habit in life that keeps your heart healthy, whole, and pure.

Fasting

Fasting, or abstaining, isn't for the purpose of making you suffer but to purify your mind, heart, and body so you can draw closer to God. Some people think fasting is only for "super Christians," but that's not true. Any of us can fast a meal to spend time in prayer for a particular need, for a day to delve more deeply into the heart of God, or for a longer time to seek God's direction for our lives. It's not about how long you fast, but about maintaining a heart connection with God. Jesus was aware that the religious leaders of His day used fasting as a measuring stick to impress people. He warned the crowds,

Moreover, when you fast, do not be like the hypocrites, with a sad countenance. For they disfigure their faces that they may appear to men to be fasting. Assuredly, I say to you, they have their reward. But you, when you fast, anoint your head and wash your face, so that you do not appear to men to be fasting, but to your Father who is in the secret place; and your Father who sees in secret will reward you openly. (Matt. 6:16–18)

Fasting is one of the quickest ways to draw closer to Him. Ask God today to enlarge your heart and begin to include fasting as part of your healthy heart habit regime.

Serving

The closer we get to God, the more He shares with us His heart for people. As you connect with God and experience His goodness and grace, He begins to use you to help others. He involves you in touching others' lives and causes you to reflect on how He has revolutionized your heart. Helping and serving others then becomes a feedback loop of grace. The Heart Revolution was always intended for your changed heart to overflow into the lives of those around you who have yet to experience the power of a turned heart. As a revolutionary, you can now live to give and love to give. Making a heart habit of serving the needs of others in your circle of influence, in the local church, and in the community keeps life, purpose, and momentum pumping through your spiritual veins.

Every new skill takes time and practice for it to become second nature, but when it becomes a habit, you don't have to try so hard anymore. Eventually you see the benefits and can't imagine a time when you didn't do those things. If you've never tapped into the power of spiritual disciplines, start today where you are. Habits of the heart become habits of your character.

It's not out of obligation or duty that these habits become part of your everyday life. It's out of a real kickin' revolution that's begun and continues in your heart. You're the real deal. Come on, somebody!

24

Stepping Up Spiritually

Spiritual maturity is marked by spiritual knowledge being put into action.

—Edward Bedore

As a father, I've watched my daughters change, mature, and rediscover themselves as they have grown through the various stages of development. I don't give a pacifier and bottle to my daughter in grade school, and I don't offer to help my oldest daughter with homework in her graduate classes. These actions would stunt their growth. Every one of my daughters is in a different place, developmentally and spiritually. As their father, I have a responsibility to know and understand where each of them is in their growth progress so that I can keep our hearts connected and encouraged. I'd be surprised and concerned if one of my teenage girls acted like a toddler.

In the same way, your heavenly Father clearly understands that you are in a process of spiritual growth, and like any good father, He applauds and encourages every step you take toward maturity. God expects every one of us to grow, become strong, and take our place as revolutionaries who are developing and maturing in Him.

Christian thinkers and scholars have identified the stages of spiritual growth in several different ways. Scripture seems to follow the simplest: infancy, adolescence, and adulthood. The problem of spiritual stagnation that was true in the early church can oftentimes still be true today. Many people never make it out of spiritual infancy. The Corinthian church was full of people who had started well but stalled along the way. In his first letter to them after he left Corinth, Paul challenged them to take an honest look at where they were spiritually:

> I have been talking to you as though you were still just babies in the Christian life, who are not following the Lord, but your own desires; I cannot talk to you as I would to healthy Christians, who are filled with the Spirit. I have had to feed you with milk and not with solid food, because you couldn't digest anything stronger. And even now you still have to be fed on milk. For you are still only baby Christians, controlled by your own desires, not God's. When you are jealous of one another and divide up into quarreling groups, doesn't that prove you are still babies, wanting your own way? (1 Cor. 3:1–3 TLB)

It's perfectly good, right, and normal for a baby to be content with milk, but eventually, the child is weaned and begins to eat solid food. With the progression of development, it's necessary and vital for a child to hunger for more than just milk. In the same respect, as you grow and develop, your needs will change. You naturally start to develop a hunger for greater revelation and truth as your image and understanding of Him grows.

Throughout your life, God will allow you to be tested to see if you're ready to move to the next level of responsibility and authority. He gives you small tasks to see if you'll trust Him and give your very best. When you do, He gives you a bigger part to play. The principle is spelled out in many different passages, but one in particular stands out:

> He who is faithful in what is least is faithful also in much; and he who is unjust in what is least is unjust also in much. (Luke 16:10)

As you trust God at each point in your development, God changes your motivations, your desires, your relationships, and your actions. Gradually, you take on more of Christ's heart. You care about the things He cares about, and what breaks His heart now breaks yours as well. When the Holy Spirit points out things in your life that displease Him, you won't shrug your shoulders in indifference, but you also won't beat yourself up with guilt when you make a mistake. You're more thankful than ever for Christ's payment for your sins, and more determined than ever to make your life count for Him. Slowly, like a child growing up in every way, your life becomes characterized increasingly by the life of the Spirit. You're more loving, more joyful, more peaceful, more patient, more kind, more dedicated to goodness, more faithful, more gentle, and less out of control of your emotions and actions (Gal. 5:22–23). That's what it means to "become more like Christ."

Why then do so many Christians stay stuck in the stage of infancy? I call it the "Baby Huey syndrome"—a heart condition that says if you play it right, you can avoid the hard work of growing up and being responsible. It's the mentality that you can enjoy all the benefits of letting others carry you without ever learning to walk yourself. But that's not the way

God wants you to live. The lifestyle of the Heart Revolution isn't self-indulgence; it's giving up your life to gain His life.

When you're tempted to try to beat the system and skip the steps of spiritual growth, know that it's the Baby Huey syndrome trying to marginalize the process of maturity that God has put in your spiritual DNA. There are no shortcuts to spiritual maturity, just as there are none for personal development in every other area of our lives. When you are willing to do what needs to be done, you become who you need to be to succeed in every stage.

The "Baby Huey syndrome"—avoiding the hard work of growing up and being responsible.

As we grow from spiritual infancy to adolescence, God prunes the areas of our life that we no longer need. Jesus compared this to pruning a grapevine:

> I am the true vine, and My Father is the vinedresser. Every branch in Me that does not bear fruit He takes away; and every branch that bears fruit He prunes, that it may bear more fruit. (John 15:1–2)

After the growing season, gardeners drastically cut back the vines. For a while, they look like nubs about knee high, but in the spring they put out new shoots, and soon, they're even more productive than the year before.

What does it look like when God prunes you? As you've been dedicated to honoring God and building His kingdom, He has used you to produce the fruit: saved people and young believers growing in their faith. Then suddenly, seemingly out of nowhere, you begin to feel your spiritual branches being cut off. The actions that were fruitful before are now unproductive. Your first reaction may be to think this is happening because you've done something wrong. But in a season of pruning, it's not your sin that caused the problem; it's actually your fruitfulness. God is taking you through the process of change and shaping so that He can make you even more fruitful in the next season. If you misunderstand what He's doing, you may be tempted to get angry with God, with yourself, and with other people. What you are perceiving as a bad thing is, in actuality, for your benefit.

As we grow, God prunes the areas of our life that we no longer need.

Pruning is never easy, but it's necessary. When I owned a landscaping business, I often pruned trees for my clients during the winter months. Many times, they came up to me after I'd finished, and even sometimes while I was in the middle of pruning their trees, and complained that I was cutting their trees back too much. I explained, "I'm not pruning them so they'll look good today. I'm thinking about what will happen in the spring and summer. I'm cutting them so that they'll look their best during the optimum growing season." I would explain that I was also pruning the cross branches in their trees so they would grow stronger and have a better shape. I was pruning with purpose and vision.

In the same way, God never prunes us haphazardly. He uses His perfect skill to cut away those parts of your life that are ineffective or unfruitful. For a while, you might look kind of sparse, but when you go through another growing season, you'll be stronger and bear more fruit than ever before. If you're growing, you can count on the fact that God will take you through times of pruning. It's part of His grand design for you.

Times of pruning most often happen at the transition points between stages. If you interpret these times correctly as beneficial, you'll continue to grow with Him. If, however, you resist these times of change and quit, your growth becomes hindered, and you remain stuck in that stage of development—until you gain new perception about what's going on and pass the test.

I'll never forget the season our church was going through years ago. We did not yet have a building, so we were forced to move our midweek service from location to location. I felt as though our church had reached a plateau, and it was a painful time for me as a pastor. I often wondered if what I was doing was really making a difference in people's lives.

At the end of this one particular Wednesday night service, I was moved by the Holy Spirit to speak to Greg, a fourteen-year-old student, who I could see was ready to give up. Greg shared with me how he felt like he had lost his passion for God and didn't know how to get it back.

"God has big plans for you! Don't stop growing!"

He had been very involved with our youth ministry for years and felt as though his season was up for doing ministry. I put both hands on his shoulders, looked him squarely in the eyes, and said, "Greg, God has not forgotten about you. You are destined for more! There's a pastor on the inside of you. Trust me, your present frustration is not your ultimate destination." I remember telling him emphatically, "God has big plans for you, Greg. Don't stop growing!" He looked up at me as though we were the only two people in the room. That conversation changed his life. He didn't give up. He did exactly what God told him to do—he kept growing. Today he is actively witnessing to other youth in our church the same message of hope and healing that caused his heart to be revolutionized! If he had stopped growing in his relationship with Christ, a vital piece of our youth ministry would be missing.

Sometimes when people face times of pruning, they incorrectly assume they can resolve the problem by changing spouses, changing jobs, changing cities, or changing churches. When they make one or more of these moves, they feel relieved for a while, but soon, old patterns of immaturity surface. It's important to recognize that we won't make progress until we pass the season of testing and pruning.

Today if you feel stuck in any area of your life, step up spiritually and begin to take steps, even baby steps, toward the next level. Don't allow your heart to be stuck any longer.

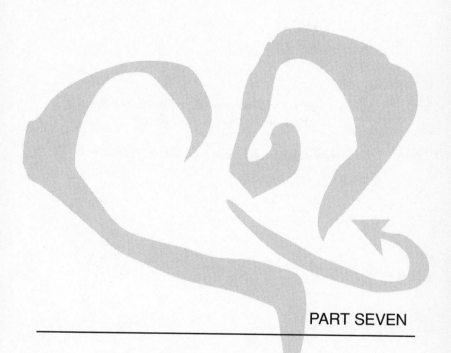

PART SEVEN

KEEPING IT REAL

Watch a special video message from Pastor Sergio
Part Seven: Keeping It Real

www.sergiodelamora.com/heartrev

25

Money: Who Controls It?

> If you want to feel rich, just count the things you
> have that money can't buy.
>
> —Anonymous

In many families, the biggest area of contention is over
who controls the purse strings. The struggle for power
over the checkbook, and more often the credit cards, can
have an enormous impact in a couple's relationship.

When I talk to couples about money, I often ask, "Who
is in charge of your family budget? Is it the man who is the
head of the family, or the wife who is the neck that turns the
head? Is it the one who has the highest credit score, the one
who finds the best bargains, the one who saves for a rainy day,
or the one who is diligent to pay the bills on time?"

In relationships, opposites attract, but after a while, those
opposites begin to *attack*. Nowhere is conflict more heated than
over how money is handled. Often, one person is a saver and the

other is a free spender, one is committed to pay the bills on time, but the other says, "Oh, it'll work out. We need it now."

So arguments erupt. As fighting escalates, some couples end up hiding their money or lying about how they spend it. The problem worsens.

Learning God's perspective on money is central to the Heart Revolution.

Our personal and family destinies are directly linked to how we handle money. When you put God in control of your money, worries about money won't control your family's destiny any longer. How then do you begin to change how money is handled in a marriage? Learning God's perspective on money is central to the Heart Revolution.

♦ **God owns it all.**

As the creator of all, God owns everything on the planet. In the Old Testament, when income was generated from ranching and farming, God declared,

> For every beast of the forest is Mine,
> And the cattle on a thousand hills. (Ps. 50:10)

We may think that the cars we drive are ours, the clothes on our backs are ours, or that the furniture we sit on is ours, but they're not. They belong to God. When we recognize the Source of our resources, which is Christ, we don't struggle with the biblical principle of tithing. Tithing is giving God back 10 percent of our income as evidence that we recognize He owns everything in our life. He doesn't want the 90 percent—only 10. Tithing is our way of boldly declaring to the world, "God, and no one else, is the One who controls my finances." And when you tithe, your money is safer than even the most well-protected investment.

The first question I ask every couple going through financial stress is, "Are you faithful tithers?" Nowhere else except in your tithe will you have a guaranteed return (Mal. 3:10). And that return overflows into every area of your life. Test God on this and get ready to see your financial situation begin to change.

Tithing is the first principle that must remain a nonnegotiable if we are going to revolutionize our finances.

◆ Our income comes from God.

I understand the argument that says, "Yeah, but my hard-earned paycheck comes from me. I am the one who gets up every morning to go to work." But who gave you the abilities, talents, brains, and opportunities? The Bible clearly tells us that our ability and power to have wealth is rooted in the One who owns everything:

> If you start thinking to yourselves, "I did all this. And all by myself. I'm rich. It's all mine!"—well, think again. Remember that God, your God, gave you the strength to produce all this wealth so as to confirm the covenant that he promised to your ancestors. (Deut. 8:17–18 Message)

It is *God* who gives us ingenuity, capabilities, and the power to create wealth, but we need to realize that all good things, including our ability to make a living, come from His hand.

◆ God has made us stewards, not owners, of money and possessions.

As we recognize that all we have is merely on loan to us from Him, we begin to see that He looks to us to be faithful stewards of His possessions. It's our job as His servants to continually ask, "How does God want me to use my money?" Ask that simple question to help you distinguish between what is a "need" and what is a "want."

◆ The way we handle money is a reflection of our hearts.

What do you think about during the day? What keeps you awake at night? The things that fill our minds are the things that have captured our hearts. Jesus warns us,

Don't save treasures for yourselves here on earth. . . . Instead, save your treasures in heaven, where they cannot be destroyed by moths or rust and where thieves cannot break in and steal them. Your heart will be where your treasure is. (Matt. 6:19–21 ESV)

Many people spend countless hours trying to figure out how to make more money, daydreaming about how to spend it, or worrying about getting a dreaded call from the collection company because they've spent too much. When our hearts are consumed with money, possessions, and debt, we have our treasures stored on earth. But when our hearts are consumed by God and those He's placed in our lives to care for, what we have will last forever.

◆ **We need to prioritize our finances.**

If we're going to be good stewards of what God has given us, we need to have a plan for the money entrusted to us. After giving God His 10 percent, give your future 10 percent as well by setting it aside in a savings account that you are committed not to touch. Make saving a core value for your family. Then begin to pay off the necessary bills such as your mortgage or rent, food, and utilities.

Most often the problem is how we prioritize our money. Planning and continually reviewing your spending habits bring accountability and partnership into your marriage. And these two elements bring unity and agreement, which in turn attracts the presence and blessings of God. Maybe you never thought of applying this basic principle to the wise use of finances in your marriage. Let me remind you of Jesus' words about the power of agreement:

[Jesus said,] "Again, I tell you that if two of you on earth agree about anything you ask for, it will be done for you by my Father in heaven. For where two or three come together in my name, there am I with them." (Matt. 18:19–20 NIV)

When people develop the disciplines of wisely saving, giving, investing, and spending, an amazing thing happens in their hearts. They know they are obeying God, so they feel closer to Him. They develop confidence in themselves, in their spouse, and in their future. Tithing is no longer a burden or an obligation, but a way to express gratitude to God and partner with Him in changing people's lives. Stress levels that were once out of control because of debt and careless spending now subside, and the whole family can enjoy a sense of peace.

Financial peace was a concept a woman in our church thought she understood well. Married for many years to a man who had given her wealth and security, Ellen had the freedom to spend the money he gave her in any way she pleased. He controlled the money, but that was fine with her because he handled the bills, mortgage, savings—everything financial. She never worried about how things got paid or when things were due, and for a period of thirty-one years, she lived in financial peace. She had the cars, the homes, the jewelry, the clothes, anything her heart could want.

Then came the day when everything changed. That morning Ellen kissed her husband goodbye, completely unaware that this would be the last day of her life as she knew it. By early evening, she received a call that her husband had been arrested. Hours after that initial call she became aware that her husband had been living a double life. It was devastating for her to learn pieces of a story about a man she thought she knew, especially because, during all the years they had been married, things were at their best. Yet here she was getting hit with the worst news of her life.

All of a sudden, it became painfully obvious that she had absolutely no idea how to handle the everyday household bills—the water bill, the gas and electric bill, the car payment, insurance. She didn't even know her bank account number. She had thirty days to pack up over three decades of "stuff" and move out of her home. She had no career, no education, and no work experience to fall back on. In one day, Ellen had literally lost everything.

It was a bleak time in her life, but she never let go of God or His plan. She stayed connected to my wife and me as her pastors and to other leaders in the church. She stayed faithful in her ministry and in her walk with God. No matter how terrifying and overwhelming the circumstances were, she refused to let them disconnect her from what God had begun doing in her life. She tithed when she had no job or money, because she knew that the only hands she could trust her finances to were God's.

She never let go of God or His plan.

The credit letters began to come in droves. Ellen dreaded getting the mail, because it was only more bills she couldn't pay. The worst envelope was the monthly IRS notice with the staggering amount of almost half a million dollars in back taxes since 1983. Worry and fear bombarded her—she would never be able to pay back that amount. Every night she would pray, "Please, God, release me from this lien."

In December 2006 I declared the word God had given me for the upcoming year: 2007—The Year of the Open Heaven. We were believing for God to pour out the deluge of heaven over our lives. Unbeknownst to Ellen, just days after I spoke that word, a letter was signed by the IRS *releasing* her from her lien in the amount of almost half a million dollars! The header on top of the letter read "Certificate of Release." Even though she doesn't have the worldly wealth she once had, she now has peace and freedom that money could never buy.

Jesus spoke more about money than any other topic when He was on earth. Was He obsessed with money? Not at all. He knew the power of money to speak to our deepest desires and capture our hearts; He knew that the love of money brings with it all kinds of problems.

Give God control over your money and choose to pursue righteousness, godliness, faithfulness, love, endurance, and gentleness (see 1 Tim. 6:10–11). See how it will revolutionize your marriage and home!

26

Sex: Love vs. Lust

It is not sex that gives the pleasure, but the lover.

—Marge Piercy, American poet

We live in a sex-saturated culture. Many people—not just men—spend hours every day fantasizing about sexual encounters. But there are differences between how men and women approach their sexual drive. Both may engage in fantasies, but generally, men want the physical pleasure and release, while women long for romance and the feeling of belonging. Few people stop to consider God's perspective about this powerful drive.

Popular author and speaker Josh McDowell observed, "The most important sex organ God created is your mind—not your body. It's control of your mind that shows your maturity. Being able to manage and control your sexual desires proves a whole lot more about your readiness than anything else you could 'prove' by letting those desires run wild. It takes guts to guard sex like a valuable diamond."[6]

One of the privileges of being a pastor is that I get the opportunity to speak into the hearts and lives of hundreds of men at our monthly men's meetings. During one of our question and answer sessions, a man raised his hand to ask a question that spoke to every man in the room. He said, "Pastor, I've been wondering. What's the difference between love and lust?"

"What's the difference between love and lust?"

"Great question," I told him. "The difference is that love gives, but lust takes."

Let's look at some important differences between the two.

♦ **Lust is about gratifying our own desires. Love delights in pleasing the other person.**

When lust dominates in a marriage, the other person often feels degraded, but with love there is always honor. Lustful thoughts focus on sexual conquests, holding power over people for our own pleasures. Our fantasies depict the most beautiful women and the most handsome men, with us as the stars of these sexual endeavors. The focus is always centered on ourselves. Love, however, fosters an active thought life without the element of such selfish desire.

Love gets enjoyment from pleasing the other person—for his or her sake. Some people perceive lust as passionate and love as bland or boring, but it doesn't have to be that way at all. Sexual expression between a husband and a wife should bring out their deepest passion for one another and inspire them to be wonderfully creative in making love. The Song of Solomon in the Bible shows that God believed sexual intimacy was one of the most rewarding and satisfying aspects of marriage.

◆ **Lust listens only to people who tell us what we want to hear. Love listens to godly advice and correction.**

People who are ensnared by lust will often go to great lengths to keep their addiction hidden. They don't want anyone pointing out where they need to change. In fact, they will many times gravitate toward other people who help them feel as though their lust is perfectly normal. But love is open to suggestions, corrections, and advice to make the relationship, not just the acts of sex, as rich and as meaningful as possible. Solomon tells us,

> The godly give good advice to their friends;
> the wicked lead them astray. (Prov. 12:26 NLT)

When we listen to what pleases our spouse, we can respond in ways that bring incredible satisfaction and fulfillment. And it's this powerful combination that brings an increase of passion and desire to the marriage bed.

◆ **When we lust, we pretend to be someone we're not. When we're in love, we're honest about who we are.**

The essence of lust is pretense. Think of all the conversations spoken in bars and clubs in an effort to get someone into bed. There's a desperation to impress the person in order to get what we want, even if it means lying to get it. But those who are committed to love are honest with themselves, with God, and with their spouse. Honesty may not feel good in the short term, but love is always established on truth, intimacy, and sincerity, not pretenses. Paul exhorts us,

> Don't just pretend to love others. Really love them. . . . Love each other with genuine affection. (Rom. 12:9–10 NLT)

Before Adam and Eve sinned, all they knew was love for one another. They had never felt shame or guilt so there was never any need to hide from God or each other. The Bible says when they sinned, they became aware of their nakedness and covered themselves.

> And as they ate [the fruit], suddenly they became aware of their nakedness, and were embarrassed. So they strung fig leaves together to cover themselves around the hips. That evening they heard the sound of the Lord God walking in the garden; and they hid themselves among the trees. The Lord God called to Adam, "Why are you hiding?" And Adam replied, "I heard you coming and didn't want you to see me naked. So I hid." (Gen. 3:7–10 TLB)

When we fall into lust, we want to do the same thing as Adam and Eve did—cover it up. But covering it up won't deal with it. It only creates an illusion that everything is fine—and an illusion will crumble. Genuineness is the foundation a strong marriage can build on for years to come.

◆ **Lust demands physical gratification. Love never forces sex. It cares enough to wait.**

The closer lustful people get to experiencing ecstasy, the more they demand satisfaction. Hormones rage, and power rules over respect and honor. But love never forces anything on the other person. Mutual consent and kindness provide an environment where both husband and wife feel secure and safe in the marriage bed. Paul wrote to the Corinthians in his famous description of love,

> Love cares more for others than for self . . .
> Doesn't force itself on others,
> Isn't always "me first." (1 Cor. 13:4–5 Message)

Aggressive or forceful behaviors open the door to fear and insecurity in a marriage, and the power of intimacy becomes hindered. When the intimacy that overflows into the rest of your marriage is hindered, other areas begin to suffer as well. But love waits. It will wait for healing when trust has been shattered. It will wait until the wedding day for intimacy. And it will wait for the heart to connect first.

♦ **Lust uses people and leaves them in worse condition than we found them. Love builds and affirms them.**

After the act, lust leaves the person feeling used and discarded. But real love does the complete opposite. Both people feel valued and adored, and the relationship brings out the best in both of them. Relationships rooted in lust often leave a person feeling uncertain and insecure about themselves. Love, on the other hand, builds the other person up from the inside out. They feel desired and needed by their spouse, not just for their physical features, but also for their inward beauty of kindness, humor, creativity, integrity, and strength. The result is a confidence in themselves, their spouse, and in their marriage.

Love builds the other person up from the inside out.

As a pastor, when my phone rings, I never know what's going to be on the other end. It could be a joyful call or it could be a sobering call. I'll never forget the day I got the call from a wife whose husband had confessed to her that he had been struggling with an addiction to pornography for years. Though they had been married for over ten years, Nancy had no idea of Victor's addiction. Until that day, she had been completely confident about their sex life. Now she began second-guessing herself, her marriage, and her husband. She shared with me the hurt, betrayal, and sadness she felt, but more than any of these emotions, I heard the confusion in her voice. She was unsure of how to deal with her pain and what to do next.

I challenged Nancy to talk to her husband about his addiction instead of shutting him out. She discovered his addiction had begun as a teenager. At the age of fifteen, Victor had started turning to pornography as an outlet for the loneliness he felt as an only child. Instead of talking about his emotions, he avoided them and covered up his addiction by turning on the computer even when he didn't want to. Over time, it became a habit that dictated his life. The saddest part was Victor's desperation to be free. The times when he turned to pornography weren't times of pleasure or satisfaction for him. They were times of suffering and anguish because he felt powerless to stop. Telling her the truth was his last hope of finally being free.

As Victor became transparent before Nancy, she began to see the torment he lived with every day, not understanding this part of himself. I remember asking her one question that shifted her focus from feeling like a victim to partner and helpmate to her husband. "Do you love him and your family enough to help him get free?"

I didn't ask Nancy if she was willing to forgive and forget. I asked her if she was willing to help heal the brokenness of her husband. If she could see that she could partner with Victor to help him overcome his addiction and keep her family together, eventually forgiveness and trust would be rebuilt. The Holy Spirit began to help her see that in her hands was the power to either help or hurt her husband. God spoke to her heart that Victor didn't need to carry the weight of more guilt on top of what he already bore. He needed to know that there was someone who would help him tear down the wall of shame. It took time and honest conversations that kept boundaries and accountability in place, but today this couple has overcome together. The power in their story isn't that Victor hasn't been tempted to turn to pornography on a computer since he confessed his secret. The power of their story is that, with the love of God and his wife, he knows that he is not powerless against addiction.

When a person is addicted to sex, pornography, and other sexual habits they question whether they can ever really be free. Like Victor, when you turn from sexual sin and give your heart to God and accept His forgiveness, you find the freedom you desperately desire. With courage and the power of the Holy Spirit to give you hope and strength, you can overcome any sexual addiction, habit, or temptation.

To help you succeed, you will need two key components in place. The first is *a covenant with God to pursue sexual purity* with your eyes, ears, mind, and heart. The second is having *an accountability partner* to help you overcome. Ideally, this should be your spouse if you're married and a trustworthy person if you are single.

Sexual sin and lust begin in the mind, but God's truth and grace revolutionize not only our thoughts, but our attitudes, and our behaviors as well. When this happens, we realize the liberating truth that we don't have to hide anymore. We are truly free.

27

Anger: Pause Before You Penalize

Anger is an acid that can do more harm to the vessel in which it is stored than to anything on which it is poured.

—Mark Twain

Years ago I counseled a family who, to all appearances, looked like the "perfect family." Jason and Karla Padilla had the house, the kids, the marriage, the cars, the careers. They even had the pedigree dog! Friends and family admired them and viewed them as the model family, an example of a life they all wanted as well. But sometimes things are not what they seem. What no one knew was that behind the doors of their picture-perfect home, this family was falling apart because of the destructive force of anger. Anyone who has ever felt or seen the effects of anger knows it has no boundaries or limits. It isn't confined to one specific community or demographic. It isn't restrained by age, religion, or any other social identity. The face of anger can touch any home, any marriage, or any heart.

In the privacy of the Padillas' home, arguments would erupt, resentment would fester, and the bitter silence would continue for weeks. Over and over Jason and Karla would lash out at one another with hurtful, sarcastic, and accusing words, unaware of the impact that each word was having on their children. He was angry. She was angry. And the kids were caught in the middle.

The Heart Revolution revolutionizes how you react when you're pushed to your limit.

Many people believe that anger, regardless of how it is expressed, is wrong. This isn't entirely accurate. Anger is a normal, God-given emotion, but when it grows into a lifestyle of uncontrollable wrath, it's wrong. It's important that we learn to differentiate between godly anger, or righteous anger, and sinful anger, or unrighteous anger. Unrighteous anger is merciless, whereas righteous anger is just. Unrighteous anger is dysfunctional and dangerous, but righteous anger is healthy and beneficial. Paul tells us,

> Go ahead and be angry. You do well to be angry—but don't use your anger as fuel for revenge. And don't stay angry. Don't go to bed angry. Don't give the Devil that kind of foothold in your life. (Eph. 4:26–27 Message)

Harboring anger in your heart and mind opens the door of your heart to the enemy and allows him to have a "place" or a "foothold." When anger, bitterness, and resentment control your heart, Satan wins. The Heart Revolution changes that by revolutionizing how you react when you're pushed to your limit. Instead of allowing anger to control us, we as revolutionaries choose to control it and pause before we respond.

Pausing allows forgiveness, grace, and mercy to prevail over wrath, anger, and rage. Sometimes we can feel exactly like this family felt. Like our homes, workplaces, or relationships are a war zone, and every day we're dodging hurtful arrows and spears of anger. Taking a moment to pause when situations start to escalate lets God remind us of His authority and power to silence the wars that can occur inside and around us, if we will only stop and be still:

> He makes wars stop from one end of the earth to the
>   other.
> He breaks every bow.
> He snaps every spear.
> He burns every shield with fire.
> He says, "Be still, and know that I am God."
> (Ps. 46:9–10 NIrV)

This moment of pause allows you to remember the greatness of who God is in your life—that He is well able to end the wars of anger, unresolved conflict, and resentment that have waged, even if it has been going on for years. If you've been the one who has experienced the wrath of another person, pausing gives God room to bring healing and restoration to you. If you've been the one struggling with anger, pausing and turning to God brings a flood of hope and strength to you so that you can overcome.

Anger, like all expressions of emotion, is an issue of the heart. Dealing with the root of anger, instead of just the fruit of it, brings the transformational change we all need and desire. Pausing allows God to expose the root and liberate you with His forgiveness so that anger no longer controls your life. Trying to deal with anger on your own may work for a little while, but if you don't resolve the problem at the heart level with Him, soon you'll either explode or implode. It's time to deal with anger head-on so that a shift can begin in your heart. *Remember, a shift in your heart brings a shift in your life.*

The unfortunate reality is, there aren't enough people taking a second to stop and think before reacting when they become overwhelmed or stressed in their workplaces, in their homes, and in their relationships. Nor are there enough people asking God to expose the root of their anger. Without these key principles, the result is often an uncontrolled outburst of rage and anger in which you end up saying and doing things you later regret. People can't thrive in an environment where anger rules. An atmosphere of anger crushes hope and cripples the potential of each person in a family, especially the ones who are most vulnerable: the children.

A shift in your heart brings a shift in your life.

As I sat in my office with this "perfect couple," I listened as Jason and Karla shared how they had gotten to this point in their relationship. After hiding their emotions for over fifteen years of marriage, both were stoic and sullen as they confronted their past for the first time. Their hearts were bitter at decisions that had been made without ever considering the other, resentful at indiscretions that had been swept under the rug, and furious at choices that had driven them farther apart. They could barely stand to be in the same room with each other. Before they could start to put the pieces of their marriage back together, they would have to first deal with the anger, but how?

Let's look at how the Padillas faced and overcame anger in their hearts and their home.

◆ **They admitted anger was a problem.**

Acknowledgment, not justification, is the first step to resolving any problem. It's always easier to blame and excuse our anger than face it, but healing always comes to the broken places first. The Bible teaches us that it's our honesty that attracts God's healing and redemption,

If we say that we have no sin, we are only fooling ourselves and refusing to accept the truth. But if we confess our sins

188

to him, he can be depended on to forgive us and to cleanse us from every wrong. (1 John 1:8–9 TLB)

It takes tremendous bravery and determination to look inward rather than outward, but when you do you begin to see how deeply anger and silence can hurt those you love. In these moments when your sin is exposed and raw, it's not the condemning voice of God that you hear. It's His gentle voice of revelation so that your heart and life are forever changed. When Karla and Jason took the revolutionary step to admit they had a problem with anger, it opened the door for genuine healing.

* **They repented to one another and to their children.**
When God exposes our weaknesses, there's always a need on our part to respond. Repentance isn't an "I'm sorry" without a heart decision to change. When we repent, we choose to walk out different behaviors, speak out different words, and live out different values. The moment we make the heart decision to turn to Him and repent, He promises that times of refreshing will follow.

So then, let your hearts be changed and be turned to God, so that your sins may be completely taken away, and times of blessing may come from the Lord. (Acts 3:19 BBE)

At first, Jason and Karla felt awkward when they paused, reflected, and expressed something other than demands, but it's like learning any new skill. In time, these new choices became new habits for them. And when they each saw the other trying to change their behaviors, they began to walk in forgiveness.

* **They recognized anger triggers.**
Every one of us has buttons or triggers that, when pressed, cause us to instantly go from irritated or annoyed to infuriated. The more you allow God to see all the pieces of your

heart, the more He reveals what to do when you feel like your buttons are being pushed. Karla and Jason took a good, long look at their pattern of anger. They took notice of the things that caused their anger button to be pushed and then began to choose alternate ways of responding. One way I suggested was for them to take a break, clear their hearts, pray, and then come back and address the issue. They weren't able to eliminate every trigger in their lives, but they learned they could overcome them.

These heart decisions, combined with God's grace, revolutionized the family that was once thought of as "perfect." Jason and Karla walked out the journey of being honest with themselves, with one another, and with their children. Did it take time, tears, and trust? Absolutely. But they did prevail. They dealt with every root, refused to give up, and gained back more than they had ever lost.

Perhaps you know very well what it feels like to be on the receiving end of anger. Or maybe you know the pain of waking up every morning, looking in the mirror, and knowing deep in your heart that you are the one struggling with anger. Whichever side you are on, if you will pause today and place your heart in God's hands, He will revolutionize how you recognize and respond to anger.

Today, God releases to you the power to heal, the courage to overcome, and the strength to try again. Let love be the dominant force in your heart. Nothing else is greater.

28

Leadership: Who Wears the Pants?

> A leader takes people where they want to go. A great leader takes people where they don't necessarily want to go, but ought to be.
>
> —Rosalynn Carter, First Lady

In every area of life, the greatest cry is for leadership. Scripture tells us,

Without wise leadership, a nation falls. (Prov. 11:14 NLT)

Everything rises and falls on leadership. If you were to trace back every problem, you would find the source is most likely a time when someone didn't take leadership. In a business, most problems arise when someone has failed to take initiative and leadership. In churches, people often struggle to connect when there's a lack of clear leadership to follow. And at home, families suffer when there's a gap in leadership. In almost every situation, leadership is the problem, and leadership is the answer.

The determining factor of success for any business, any relationship, any church, any student, any couple, and any family, is the willingness to take responsibility for the conditions that have either been created or need to be created. Jesus said,

> You are the salt of the earth. But suppose the salt loses its saltiness. How can it be made salty again? It is no longer good for anything. It will be thrown out. People will walk all over it. (Matt. 5:13 NIrV)

He wasn't talking to people who looked or sounded like leaders. They struggled with low self-esteem, fear, and insecurity. No one viewed them as elite, favored, or even qualified. Yet here's Jesus speaking these revolutionary words to them, calling them world changers, influencers, and leaders. He called them the salt of the earth, meaning they have been purposed to preserve, season, and create thirst in the earth. His message to them was, regardless of the atmosphere they were in, they were called to penetrate and change it.

God calls you the salt of the earth—a leader.

The same is true today. God calls you the salt of the earth— a leader. You have been chosen and equipped to preserve the lives of others, to season their hearts with passion and purpose, and to create in them a thirst for God. You already have the potential and ability within you to lead. The Bible says that all you have to do is step up and go for it:

> If God has given you leadership ability, take the responsibility seriously. (Rom. 12:8 NLT)

All of us are faced with the decision every day to either be a leader or a follower. There are opportunities in every avenue of your life to either sit back and say nothing or stand up and say something. In times of change and crisis, your world is waiting, hoping that you will step up and be an influencer. Your co-workers, your family, your friends, and your church are believing that you'll step up with a boldness that is courageous and honest, not explosive or overly aggressive. The kind of leadership that will step in and say the things that need to be said and do the things that need to be done in order to bring peace, order, and authority.

I remember a walk I had with a young up-and-coming leader during our summer youth camp. Alex was a good-looking, successful businessman who commanded million-dollar accounts at work. But at home, it was his wife who commanded everything. There are some questions you should only ask if you are willing and ready to hear the answer. That day he asked me one such question. Alex wanted to get more involved at church and asked me, "Pastor, what does it take to be a leader? What do you think I need to do?"

I took this opportunity to talk to him privately about something I had noticed. If there was ever a moment I was going to address it, the moment was now. With guys, there are some conversations that can only happen in the confines of two men. Maybe it was the heat or maybe it was the fatigue of taking 250 youth to the beach—whatever it was, I looked at this guy who was three times my size and said, "Alex, do you really want to know?"

He nodded, looking unsure of what was coming next.

I stopped walking and challenged him, "If you want to be in leadership, you need to start wearing the pants in your family, because up until now your wife has worn the pants. She's obviously more spiritual than you. You need to step up at home if you want to step up here."

I didn't know how he was going to react to my blunt honesty, but the look on his face read, "Who do you think you are?"

I'm sure he expected a three-point sermon on how to get involved at church, but that wasn't what he got. No, Alex got an honest, man-to-man conversation about the reality of leadership in a marriage. As a result of that conversation, he began to make changes in his marriage that altered the trajectory of his home. Alex took spiritual ownership of the atmosphere in his home and began praying and reading his Bible without the direction or nudge of his wife.

You are a thermostat— not a thermometer—of leadership.

Instead of feeling angry or resentful at the shift in her husband, his wife was grateful for the restoration of order. She felt relieved not to have the pressure of making leadership decisions, and he felt honored in her willingness to follow his lead. How refreshing it is to see that today he wears the pants both at home and in ministry.

Even if you feel like you've lost your right to lead, it's time to do what this man did and start operating as a leader today. You are a thermostat—not a thermometer—of leadership. A thermometer merely tells the condition of the atmosphere, but a thermostat changes it!

Job understood what it was like to feel as though he had lost his right to lead. He endured more than anyone can imagine, but through it all, he never gave up on God or on his role as a leader. He reminded his friends of his commitment to lead, even in the midst of painful conditions:

> I was their leader, establishing the mood
> and setting the pace by which they lived.
> Where I led, they followed. (Job 29:25 Message)

There are places in your life that need your leadership today. Let's look at what happens when you step up to lead in the home, at work, and at church:

♦ **At home, God restores the ordained roles in the family and establishes order and peace.**

Leadership at home can often be the most difficult place to set the mood because the ordained roles of the family have been altered and become confusing. Roles in a family aren't up for debate. They've been clearly established by God. He has given husbands and fathers the crucial role of leading. When they take this responsibility, anything is possible for a family. When they abdicate this role, everyone is affected and the result can be painful. Paul reminds us of these roles:

> For the husband is head of the wife, as also Christ is head of the church; and He is the Savior of the body. Therefore, just as the church is subject to Christ, so let the wives be to their own husbands in everything. (Eph. 5:23–24)

Submission isn't hard when proper leadership is in place. When men function effectively as strong, loving leaders, women want to acknowledge and agree to their leadership. And when there is proper leadership in place, children have a sense of peace at home, even when change and crisis occur. The roles of husband and wife, and mother and father, are the most important leadership positions God can give us.

What happens if you've made wrong leadership decisions in the past and aren't sure how to reestablish your right to lead? Start today to lead again. Remember that you can't command your family to trust your leadership—you have to earn it. By the right blend of tenderness and toughness, flexibility and firm direction, you can show your spouse and children that they can trust your leadership. When you work to make this happen, everyone wins at home. And when you win at home, you'll win everywhere.

♦ **At work, our leadership inspires others and glorifies God.**

Whether you're the boss or the employee, leadership in business is vital. The workplace is not just where you go to put in forty hours to receive a paycheck. At every workplace, you have the opportunity to do your best and develop your God-given potential. As a boss, it's your leadership that inspires your employees to strive for greater things. As an employee, it's your leadership that allows the company to operate in the fullness of its vision and purpose.

Too many people view their jobs as "work" and miss the opportunity to demonstrate a spirit of excellence on the job to the world around them. Jesus Christ is our first boss, and when we aim to do our best for Him at our workplace, we will be doing our best for our earthly boss. We, as Christians, are called to be the best leaders in our jobs, because we serve the One who gives us all power and authority to do anything we are asked (Phil. 4:13). He is looking to us to have the strongest testimonies at work so that He can be glorified. In practicality, this means being on time, on task, and on purpose in all we do.

Consider the words of the Bible to encourage you to have the right perspective at work:

> Don't just do the minimum that will get you by. Do your best. Work from the heart for your real Master, for God, confident that you'll get paid in full when you come into your inheritance. Keep in mind always that the ultimate Master you're serving is Christ. The sullen servant who does shoddy work will be held responsible. Being a follower of Jesus doesn't cover up bad work. (Col. 3:22–25 Message)

◆ At church, our leadership fulfills the mission and vision of Jesus.

It was leadership that established the church and leadership that preserves the church, enabling us to fulfill the final command Jesus spoke to His disciples:

> All authority has been given to Me in heaven and on earth. Go therefore and make disciples of all the nations, baptizing them in the name of the Father and of the Son and of the

Holy Spirit, teaching them to observe all things that I have commanded you; and lo, I am with you always, even to the end of the age. (Matt. 28:18–20)

When we as a church body take a leadership role in our communities, we bring the revolution outside the doors of the church and into the hearts of the people. On a personal level, when you operate as a leader who gets involved, takes ownership of the mission of your church, and commits to raising the next generation, you carry out God's purpose and mission on earth. Your leadership makes all the difference.

It takes courage and tenacity to lead, to do the right thing, and to give your life as a sacrifice for those you love day in and day out. It takes discipline and focus to set the pace for those around you. But most importantly, it takes a heart that won't be defined by decisions in the past—a heart determined to lead. Don't wait for anyone else to set the temperature of leadership. Your leadership makes all the difference.

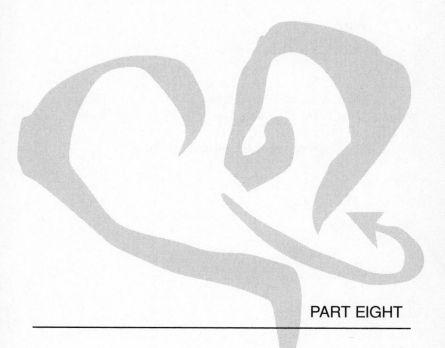

TURNING YOUR HEART TOWARD HOME

Watch a special video message from Pastor Sergio
Part Eight: Turning Your Heart toward Home

www.sergiodelamora.com/heartrev

29

Listen with Your Heart, Not Just Your Head

No one is as deaf as the man who will not listen.

—Jewish Proverb

Home is where the heart is." If home is where the heart is and the heart is where the Heart Revolution begins, it stands to reason that this revolution must impact our homes before it can permeate beyond the front door. For many people, though, home is the place where they feel the least like a winner. Strained relationships, broken promises, and selfish behaviors have torn down the foundation of too many homes. One glance at the condition of families today shows that too many of them are experiencing the effects of broken relationships.

Bitterness, division, unresolved conflict, isolation, anger, and complacency are just some of the issues families in our society are dealing with. The aim of the Heart Revolution is to bring healing and restoration to families by getting to the root of these issues. When our hearts become revolutionized by God, we stop trying to hide or numb what's truly in them. Then we can approach issues in our families with an openness and willingness to see genuine restoration occur. God not only wants strained and broken relationships at home to experience His healing; He longs for it. The very last words of God in the Old Testament describe His heart for family restoration:

One trait is crucial to keeping our hearts turned: *listening* to one another.

> And he will turn
> The hearts of the fathers to the children,
> And the hearts of the children to their fathers,
> Lest I come and strike the earth with a curse. (Mal. 4:5–6)

As we turn our hearts toward our families, the course of our relationships begins to change. One trait above all else is crucial to keeping our hearts turned toward Him and each other: *listening* to one another.

We live in an auditory society. Culturally, we are constantly being exposed to the continuous hum of modern life. As a result, there is a propensity to become so plugged in to devices that many of us have lost the art of listening to one another. Our relationships, however, become transformed when we create a culture of listening. Your ear is the gateway to your heart. When you learn to hear a person's heart behind their words, you discover that communication becomes clearer, richer, and more meaningful. Listening brings a connection to one another on a heart level.

It's imperative we learn to listen with our hearts and not just with our heads. When we listen with our heads, we gather only enough facts and information for the moment, but we become deaf to the unspoken messages, the ones that are most important. Listening with your heart is both an art and a science. As you pay attention to the unspoken messages found in facial expressions and tone of voice, you begin to relate to and connect with the people you love the most.

Gaining God's perspective on what someone is saying changes everything.

Most communication problems between husband and wife or parent and child are rooted in listening solely from the head. Head listening will only give you partial information, often leading to misunderstandings and assumptions. Assumptions breed resistance and resentment, because the other person often feels you are more concerned with your own agenda than their heart, which causes them to withdraw from you. Gaining God's perspective on what they are saying changes everything. He brings truth to areas of miscommunication and tempers assumptions with His humility.

Here are some suggestions on how to listen on a heart level:

◆ **Ask God for wisdom.**

When you seek God's wisdom, He reveals to you that, in every conversation between parents and children or husband and wife, there aren't just two people present. There are three. God is ever present, waiting to help guide our words and thoughts so that we can listen from our hearts. Begin to depend on the unseen third party as you communicate to your family, and ask God for direction.

> If any of you lacks wisdom, let him ask of God, who gives to all liberally and without reproach, and it will be given to him. (James 1:5)

◆ Listen before you speak.

Have you ever met someone whose mouth was constantly in the "on" position? People like this can't stop telling others what they think, how they feel, and what they think you should do. Communication that brings healing will always include pauses and moments of reflection. When we speak without pausing, we tend to say things we don't mean or respond in ways we don't intend. The Bible teaches us,

> Be swift to hear, slow to speak, slow to wrath; for the wrath of man does not produce the righteousness of God. (James 1:19–20)

◆ Learn to ask good questions.

Genuine communication always involves asking open-ended questions that invite people to give their opinions, thoughts, and emotions. Questions that aren't dependent on a right or wrong response are less intimidating. For example, ask, "What did you think about . . . ?" or "How do you think that happened?" One of the best things to say to follow up an answer is the simple but effective request, "Tell me more about that." This lets them know you're not only hearing them, you're engaged with them.

◆ Listen with empathy.

Body language many times will say more than what is actually spoken. Our words make up only 7 percent of our communication. The other 93 percent is our gestures, facial expressions, and body language. We communicate empathy when we look the person in the eye, nod occasionally, and sit back in our chairs to show we're relaxed. Families that have the confidence of knowing someone wants to hear what they have to say will be more likely to communicate when a conflict arises. Your body language and responses say, "I'm here and I want to know what you're thinking."

◆ **Choose the right time to speak.**

Not every moment is the right moment to speak. Sometimes it's best to wait and regroup your thoughts so you can be clear in what you want to say. The best moments are usually those that aren't filled with distractions or when emotions are at their peak. The Bible says,

> Say the right thing at the right time and help others by what you say. (Eph. 4:29 CEV)

Setting time aside to communicate openly and honestly allows the other person to see that you value communication and reconciliation.

◆ **Choose words that build up, not destroy.**

Our words have incredible power to bring life or death (Prov. 18:21). As you learn to listen with your heart, the people around you will begin to open up and become more vulnerable. As they feel respected and understood, they begin to give you access into their hearts. In those tender moments, walk carefully. The goal of all our conversations is to build up, restore, and support. Speak life, hope, and faith in your conversations and the door of communication will always remain open. Paul's reminder to us keeps us grounded and purposeful in our words:

> Let no corrupt word proceed out of your mouth, but what is good for necessary edification, that it may impart grace to the hearers. (Eph. 4:29)

I would have to admit that, in general, women are better listeners than men. To be truthful, I would say the majority of us men struggle to communicate and listen. One particular father I remember came to me after service and told me blatantly, "Your church doesn't work."

After getting over my initial shock, I asked him what he meant.

Steven began to tell me that he had been bringing his wife and kids to church for six months but had seen no change in his relationship with them. He told me of his strained relationship with his teenage son. In so many words, Steven was basically accusing me of not "fixing" his relationship with his family. I admired his boldness and began to ask him what he thought the root problem was with his son. He opened up that they had never had a real conversation with one another. I could see his frustration with the situation and asked him one more question. "Have you ever told your son you loved him?"

When you listen with your heart, you look beyond the words and past surface emotions.

He looked at me like I was crazy and said, "His mother tells him enough. That's her job."

For the next two hours, I sat with Steven and began to help him see the powerful role God had given him in his son's life. We picked through every act of rebellion his son was demonstrating that in actuality was really a cry for his approval and love. Once he learned to stop hearing only what was coming out of his son's mouth, Steven started to hear what was coming out of his heart and things began to change.

In every relationship, when you focus on listening with your heart, you look beyond the words and past surface emotions. It's in this way the Bible says that you will begin to rebuild the foundation of your home:

> Through skillful and godly Wisdom is a house (a life, a home, a family) built, and by understanding it is established [on a sound and good foundation], and by knowledge shall its chambers [of every area] be filled with all precious and pleasant riches. (Prov. 24:3–4 AMP)

Today, as you turn your heart toward your home and begin to build on the foundation of God's wisdom, the understanding of His Word, and the knowledge of His love and purpose for your family, you will begin to see the Heart Revolution become alive and active throughout your home.

How you communicate with those you love is only one avenue to see change happen in your home. Press in during your time of prayer today and begin to ask God for wisdom and direction to approach the issues that arise in your conversations. As He begins to reveal the areas that need healing and reconciliation, be quick to respond. Keep your ears open to all that He desires to deposit into your heart. He may begin to speak through your spouse or your children about situations that need to be turned back to Him and to your family. Today, be a revolutionary and heal the heart of your family by choosing to listen, not just from your head, but from your heart.

30

The Miracle in Your Marriage

You don't marry someone you can live with, you
marry someone you cannot live without.

—Anonymous

When two people say "I do," something miraculous
occurs. The two become one:

"For this reason a man will leave his father and
mother and be united to his wife, and the two will become
one flesh" So they are no longer two, but one. (Matt. 19:5–6
NIV)

God takes two different people, with two different personalities, two different backgrounds, and two different ideals,
and produces oneness. It's this mystifying union of two people
that tells the world these two individuals are now united,
connected, intertwined, and woven together by His grace.

Jesus continued to speak profound words about the grace required for marriage:

> Not everyone is mature enough to live a married life. It requires a certain aptitude and grace. Marriage isn't for everyone. . . . But if you're capable of growing into the largeness of marriage, do it. (Matt. 19:11 Message)

Marriage is a great mystery, and one we continue to explore throughout our married lives. Becoming one begins at the altar, but making it a reality in our everyday life is a lifelong process.

Along the journey, the pressures of married life begin to do one of two things: drive you closer to one another or drive you apart. If you will allow the pressure to bring you closer together, the result is a partnership that can withstand even the most challenging situations.

Becoming one begins at the altar, but making it a reality is a lifelong process.

Georgina and I understand what it means to live under pressure all too well. Not only do we understand the same pressures that every marriage goes through, but we also understand the pressure of living a very public life. We've learned over years of pastoring together that it takes a mega-marriage to grow a mega-church. As the church and the influence God has given us has grown, more and more people have begun to look to our marriage as a model.

Like all couples, we've gone through seasons when one of us was discouraged and needed the approval and affirmation of the other to lift us up. Without both of us being committed to the miracle in our marriage, we could have drifted apart during times of stress. But instead, our marriage and love for one another has grown stronger as a result of our commitment to maintain our partnership.

Years ago, though I knew God was calling me to start a church, I was torn between God's calling and my doubts. I wrestled with this decision for a long time, and I was on the verge of saying no to God. I'll never forget the night Georgina and I stayed up for hours talking about the pros and cons of moving from Santa Barbara to San Diego. I shared with her all my doubts and fears of taking our family from the comfort of everything we'd ever known to start a church in a city where no one knew us. In a moment of vulnerability, I asked her, "Who would come to my church? Who would want to come hear me preach?"

I borrowed her yes when all I had was a no.

She looked into my eyes and said with more conviction than I'd ever heard in her voice before, "I would go to your church. I would go to hear you preach!"

At a point when I didn't believe in myself, Georgina believed in me. She saw God's calling on my life, and I borrowed her yes when all I had was a no.

Sometimes when all you have is a no, you have to do what I did and borrow your spouse's yes. When you feel like you can't be the parent you need to be, or you can't keep going another day at your job, or you can't imagine being free from debt, you need to tap into the faith of your spouse and borrow their faith. Suppose your spouse doesn't have a yes on the inside of them either. What do you do then? You borrow God's yes until you can be the yes for them! Don't ever let a no stop your marriage from fulfilling its God-given potential. Be a partner to your spouse today and watch your marriage grow in miraculous ways.

I've counseled hundreds of couples who have stopped partnering with one another because they've decided to pursue their own happiness and fulfillment instead of remembering marriage is a place of honor, servanthood, and respect. Building a marriage of partnership requires both of you to take a stand against one of the greatest hindrances—selfishness. Selfishness is like sand in the gears of a marriage. When one person insists on pursuing their own happiness above the needs of their spouse, the inner components of your relationship grind, and friction creates hot anger and resentment until eventually the movement and vitality of the marriage comes to a halt. You can stop selfishness from taking root in your marriage by identifying, acknowledging, and repenting from any area of self-fulfillment.

When you take the revolutionary step to confront the innermost desires of your heart, you find the strength from God to change and begin to see rewards in your marriage you never could have imagined. Finding the miracle in your marriage rekindles the fire of romance, restores respect, reestablishes God in the center of your marriage, and reproduces more miracles in your relationships.

Let's take a closer look at these rewards that come from putting the miracle of oneness back in your marriage.

◆ Oneness rekindles the fire of romance.

Romance isn't just about flowers, chocolate, and candlelit dinners for two. True romance is meeting the other's needs above your own, which creates an atmosphere of transparency and intimacy. When our marriages are transparent and honest, we enjoy each other's company, and get excited to express our passion and affection in tender, intimate ways. It can be rekindled by simple gestures such as opening a car door for your wife, holding your husband's hand, or giving a card for no special occasion at all. If it's been a long time since you've done something thoughtful for your spouse, go out today and do something for them that tells them, "I'm thinking about you." You'll see that the reward will far surpass the investment.

◆ Oneness restores respect.

Without respect, our marriages become vulnerable to verbal and emotional attacks. Respect is what protects a marriage from one person saying and doing things without regard for the other person. When you take steps to put the miracle of oneness back in your marriage, you erase the fear and hostility that often come when a husband or wife has felt the sting of disrespect. Respect will flow freely in a marriage where both partners value and honor each other's worth.

◆ **Oneness reestablishes God in the center of the marriage.**

It's clear from the teachings of Jesus, Paul, Peter, and others in the Bible that God never meant to put couples together and send them off to make it work on their own without Him. He wants to be in the center of the couple's life together. Every marriage experiences a range of ups and downs that remind us of our need of Him. In the difficulties of life, we realize we need God more than ever, and in the good times, we recognize that He gives us every good gift. In every season our marriages go through, we need Him at the center to give us perspective, strength, and hope.

◆ **Oneness reproduces more miracles in the relationship.**

God delights in pouring out abundance into our marriages. Couples who sow love and respect reap a rich harvest of passion, joy, strength, and wisdom—a clear example of God's law of sowing and reaping. Even more powerful is that this harvest multiplies in other relationships, such as with your kids and other couples. Begin to sow seeds of romance, respect, and reverence for God, and His Word promises you will reap far more than you sowed.

How does an individual or a couple begin to put the miracle back into their marriage and see these rewards? The first step is always to break the code of silence. Many people sit back and wait for the other person to take the first step. But passivity is dangerous. Jesus never healed a marriage during His ministry on earth. He healed people who then went on to heal their marriages. It's a process with beautiful results, well worth the time and effort.

Whatever it takes, make the first move, and watch for a miracle to begin.

31

Respect: The Glue
That Keeps You Together

There is no respect for others without humility
in one's self.

—Henri Frédéric Amiel, philosopher and poet

Aretha Franklin struck a chord that resonates in all of us when she sang, "R-E-S-P-E-C-T. Find out what it means to me." As a DJ, I always knew the right moment to play this song at a dance or party. Very few songs evoke the same emotion as this anthem. That is because one of the greatest needs in our relationships is respect.

In a marriage, we crave words of affirmation from our spouse that make us feel valued and wanted. When it's absent, the heart connection, the glue that holds us together, begins to erode. The adhesive that brings unity, agreement, security, and confidence is found in our level of respect for

213

one another. Love and respect go hand in hand in marriage. The outpouring of both demonstrates that you honor the presence of God in the other person.

When we don't honor God's presence and His work in our spouses, we fail to affirm who He has called them to be, we violate what He is doing in their lives and, as a result, make our marriages unfruitful. Take for example David's wife Michal. Their marriage started out with great promise.

Love and respect go hand in hand in marriage.

David was the great warrior who had defeated Goliath, the Israelites' greatest enemy. Michal was the daughter of Saul, the first king to rule in Israel. And yet, the pedigree of their past could not guarantee the success of their marital future, because a healthy marriage requires more than a prestigious pedigree. It requires mutual respect.

When David began to celebrate and praise God with zeal for his victory over the Philistines, Michal despised his enthusiasm for God to the point that she made a decision in her heart to hate him.

> [David] danced in the sight of the Lord with all his might. He did it while he was bringing up the ark of the Lord. The whole community of Israel helped him bring it up. They shouted. They blew trumpets.
>
> The ark of the Lord was brought into the City of David. Saul's daughter Michal was watching from a window. She saw King David leaping and dancing in the sight of the Lord. That made her hate him in her heart. (2 Sam. 6:14–16 NIrV)

What caused Michal to hate her husband was a lack of respect. I imagine it was difficult for her to celebrate the new things God was doing through David now, instead of her father. I'm sure she struggled with the changes David represented both in Israel and in her life personally. The result of Michal's disrespect for David was tragic.

Saul's daughter Michal didn't have any children as long as she lived. (2 Sam. 6:24 NIrV)

The hatred and contempt in her heart directly affected David and Michal's inability to produce a child. Moreover, what's interesting is Scripture does not refer to Michal as David's wife but rather as Saul's daughter. Could it be that Michal never transitioned her heart to respect and honor David as her husband and king? Perhaps it was because her family never valued or honored David that she took on their sentiment rather than respect and celebrate the marriage God had given her. Because the condition of your heart will always determine the course of your life, Michal was recorded simply as Saul's daughter, not as David's wife.

David and Michal's story stands as a warning to marriages today. Too many couples are struggling to see fruit in their marriage and children because of unresolved disrespect. Even if you don't like what your spouse is doing at the moment, you can still respect the presence of God in their life because Christ is at work in every situation. And this warning isn't only for wives, but husbands also. When we demonstrate respect for our spouses, it protects us not only from unfruitful marriages, but unfruitful prayers as well:

Husbands, in the same way be considerate as you live with your wives, and treat them with respect as the weaker partner and as heirs with you of the gracious gift of life, so that nothing will hinder your prayers. (1 Peter 3:7 NIV)

The Bible challenges us to see our spouses as heirs with us. Seeing your husband or wife from this perspective allows you to realize their eternal value. Each person has been created by the God of the universe for His purpose and has been given an eternal destiny beyond comparison. When you recognize that, you're able to look at your spouse and others through a different lens and treat them with the utmost respect.

When you learn to protect and respect God's call on your life as a couple, it becomes easier for you to treasure, cherish, and honor each other. It's this perspective—God's perspective—that protects your marriage and family from ever feeling demoralized, devalued, and defeated.

Seeing your spouse as an heir with you allows you to realize their eternal value.

These words—demoralized, devalued, and defeated—described Sandra perfectly. She was ready to give up and walk away from her marriage of over twenty years because she had lost all respect for her husband. After multiple acts of infidelity with other women that produced a child as a result of one of the affairs, Sandra had had enough. She was ready to walk out of my office and head straight to the courthouse to file divorce papers. I took a deep breath and told Sandra what God had told me for her marriage: "Don't sign divorce papers yet. Give me thirty days." Sandra looked at me, emotionless, and said, "Pastor, it's going to take more than thirty days to repair the disrespect he has caused in my family." I challenged her to try again, reminding her, "It took over twenty years to get here. You need a window of hope, Sandra. These next thirty days are a window of hope for God to do a miracle in your marriage."

Those thirty days started this couple on their road to recovery. Of all the marital problems, the road to recovery after disrespect has occurred is the longest and most painful. A gamut of raw emotions needed to be healed over time. Their road to recovery was more than they could handle on their own. They needed a mediator to help them put in place stringent accountability so that the reservoir of respect could begin to flow again. They made the courageous decision to see a professional Christian counselor. There were years and years of shame, regret, fear, anger, and sadness that needed to be tackled and confronted, and they couldn't do it alone. And they needed more than healing for themselves; they needed to help their children heal the wounds of their past as well. It took over a year of professional counseling for Sandra to finally begin to feel as though she had made the right decision not to pursue divorce that day. Every day for this couple was a fight for truth and love.

I want to tell you it was easy for them, but it wasn't. It took every ounce of faith they had in God and in each other to walk down that road of recovery together. But they did it. Eventually they rediscovered the glue of love, honor, and respect that had once held them together. When I look at this family now, I am reminded of the Scripture,

> Unfailing love and truth have met together.
> Righteousness and peace have kissed. (Ps. 85:10 NLT)

Today, if you feel like you're ready to give up on your marriage, wait. Give yourself a window of hope for God to do a miracle. Ask God to help you see your relationships with eyes of love and respect instead of anger or hate. His Word promises He will cover your hurt, offense, and pain.

> Hatred stirs up strife,
> but love covers all sins. (Prov. 10:12)

If you will trust in God and take the courageous steps on your own road to recovery, He will make the crooked places straight again and the rough places smooth (Isa. 40:4). Hold His Word and His promises in high regard, and you'll begin to see Him transfer your respect for Him to all of your relationships. Your marriage can make it!

32

Inspiring the Hearts
of Your Children

The great man is he that does not lose his child's
heart.

—Mencius, Chinese philosopher

Poet John Wilmot once said, "Before I got married, I had
six theories about bringing up children; now I have six
children and no theories." Raising children can be our
greatest joy and our greatest challenge as well. We cherish and
love them, but they test us in ways that nothing else could.

The Heart Revolution isn't just for you and for your marriage. It is meant to revolutionize the way you relate to your
children. Your children, or future children, are the barometer
of your heart. They reflect how much you've tapped into
God's love, forgiveness, and power, and call us on the carpet

when we waver from authentic faith. Kids are brutally honest when it comes to what they see.

My girls have always helped to keep me grounded by their honesty. Every morning I take my daughters to school and we have some of the most powerful conversations on our morning ride. My kids don't hold back their thoughts or opinions. They will tell me straight out, for example, if they didn't like the way I preached a point from my sermon the day before. By the same token, they will give me their approval when something really impacts them. And most of the time, they're right. I cherish those moments with them, and I often leave these conversations more fired up about how to be a better husband, father, and pastor.

The Heart Revolution is meant to revolutionize the way you relate to your children.

In our society, God has instituted environments for our children to learn and grow strong, but home remains their primary source of truth, love, and direction. We, as parents, play the most important role in a child's life.

Throughout their formative years, kids will instinctively ask their parents two crucial questions. They may not verbalize these exact words, but their hearts long for parents to give them the answers to "Who am I?" and "What really matters in life?" To the degree that we answer these questions well is the degree our children will grow up emotionally, spiritually, and relationally healthy.

On those rides to school every morning, as my girls jump out of the car to start their day, I tell them the same thing every single day: "Be a leader, not a follower today. I love you."

Today, they stand on those words. When they don't know which way to go or what to do, they share with me that they remember my words to them. Parents are kickin' powerful!

When we look at the life of Jesus, we're given a wonderful example of speaking words of affirmation at a point of transition in a child's life. Matthew tells us about the moment when John the Baptist met Jesus at the Jordan:

When He had been baptized, Jesus came up immediately from the water; and behold, the heavens were opened to Him, and He saw the Spirit of God descending like a dove and alighting upon Him. And suddenly a voice came from heaven, saying, "This is My beloved Son, in whom I am well pleased." (Matt. 3:16–17)

This was a turning point in Jesus' life. He was about to embark on His mission to rescue the world, but first He needed to hear His Father's approval. At that moment, His Father stopped everything in heaven to talk to His Son.

What was the Father's message? He spoke words of love and affirmation, which gave His Son confidence for the future. In one statement, the Father told Jesus who He was and communicated His heartfelt emotions. It's a beautiful example of how powerful the words of a parent are in the life of a child. All children live to hear the same words from their parents.

When we speak to our children, there are three important statements they need to hear us say. We need to say them often, clearly, and powerfully. They are:

- "I love you."
- "I'm proud of you."
- "You're good at . . ."

Saying "I love you" once isn't enough, for spouses or for kids. Children are fragile and they need tons of reassurance, especially when they face new challenges in their lives. We need to tell them often and tell them well. When they are teenagers, they may shrug their shoulders and roll their eyes when we offer words of affirmation and approval, but that doesn't mean they aren't listening or that they don't need to hear it.

Most often, this is the time when they need it most. Teenagers face the biggest tests in life every day at home and at school. Their job is to figure out who they are, where they are going, and who they want to spend time with for the rest of their lives. They may look like they don't want to hear our words of love and encouragement, but they do. They look to you as their example, their inspiration, and their model. Your words inspire them to reach for the stars and become heroes to themselves and to those around them.

Ask God to show you where your children need your approval the most.

Your words, though, must be sincere. Fake affirmation is worse than none at all. If you're having a hard time finding a character quality to affirm in your child, begin to spend time with them and ask questions about their world. As they open up to you, ask God to show you where they need your approval the most. It's there. You just have to look to find it. Then speak words that impart your faith, your excitement, and your belief in them with all your heart, trusting God to penetrate even a resistant heart.

Psychologists have identified particular stages of human development, from infancy to old age. The bridges between these stages are "rites of passage"—times when the child feels uncertain and vulnerable. If parents understand the challenge and threat of the next stage in their child's life, they can help them take a bold step of growth. Your children need your affirmation all the time, but especially at those crucial moments. They need you to step boldly into their lives to speak wisdom, confidence, and faith about the future. The Bible says,

> Point your kids in the right direction—
> when they're old they won't be lost. (Prov. 22:6
> Message)

As you've seen throughout this book, I owe my life to my parents who inspired me every day by their words and example to be a better man. They encouraged me to dream big dreams, to work hard to make those dreams come true, to love people with genuine affection, and to be faithful to my family always.

That didn't mean they would hesitate to use hard truths to inspire me when necessary. When I was in a gang, I needed a vision for my life, and my parents could see that. They had a script for my life, but I needed their words and vision to help me find my way to live it out.

Modeling is the most powerful teaching tool in the world.

I will never forget one day when my father picked me up after school in his landscaping business truck and spoke to me as only a father can. On the way home, he parked the truck in front of a cemetery. I thought it was odd, but then he turned to me and said, "Sergio, what do you see?"

I told him, "A cemetery."

"What's in a cemetery?" he asked.

I replied sarcastically, "Dead people, Dad. What else do you see at a cemetery?"

He asked, "When did they die?"

"I don't know," I told him in a frustrated tone of voice. "It says on their tombstones."

"No," he told me. "Most of these people died long before that."

He paused for a second, and then he told me a truth that I always remember even to this day: "Sergio, if you don't have a vision for your life, you're already dead."

That conversation with my father lifted the lid off my life. His words gave me the vision I was lacking and inspired me to get out of the gang and believe I was born for more. Our talk that day didn't happen by chance. My father had been planning it for a long time.

Some of us may be tempted to say we can't inspire our kids because our own parents were harsh or distant. Modeling is the most powerful teaching tool in the world, but when you and I stand before God, He's not going to ask us what kind of model our parents were for us. He's going to ask us what kind of model we were for our kids.

Even if divorce or addiction or rage or any other problem goes back generation after generation in your family, today is the day to break the devastating cycle of the past and inaugurate a new model for your children, for your children's children, and for generations to come. Begin with an honest appraisal of your relationship with your kids. Don't blame them, don't blame your parents, and don't blame your spouse. Take ownership of your attitude and behavior, and decide to turn your heart back to God and back to your family. They need you. If you will stand in the gap for them and model for them what to do, they will follow. Be their hero today and watch as they become your heroes as well.

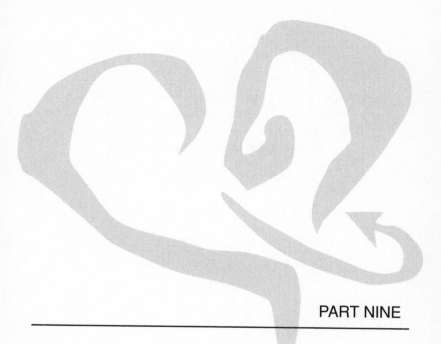

PART NINE

TURNING THE
HEARTS OF OTHERS

Watch a special video message from Pastor Sergio
Part Nine: Turning the Hearts of Others

www.sergiodelamora.com/heartrev

33

Never Forget Where You Came From

A person who forgets where he came from is a person who has forgotten his purpose.

—Anonymous

At Cornerstone Church of San Diego, every empty seat is an empty heart that God wants to fill. For us, every empty seat serves as a monument of our commitment to continue to "turn the hearts of youth and families." This is because every single one of us, including myself, remembers what it felt like to come to church for the first time and sit in an empty chair. It's what keeps our heart fresh and on fire for God.

In fact, inside the doors of our café is an encased green plastic chair from our first services at Hilltop High School that serves as a constant reminder of where we first began.

Every one of my assistant pastors and staff at one time sat in that green plastic chair and made the decision to turn their heart to Christ. It's there to remind us that no matter how far we go for God, we will never forget where we came from. As long as there are empty seats, there will still be hearts to turn. Evangelism is in our veins, our blood, our lifeline because we purposely fight to never forget what it feels like to need to be rescued. What keeps the heartbeat of this revolution alive is our thirst to see more souls saved for the kingdom of God. This is why we strategically plan over ten outreaches a year.

Remember what it felt like to have an empty heart.

When we began to see the effects of the economy in our yearly budget, it was our outreach and marketing budget that took the hit. In my time of prayer I asked God for a divine strategy to continue to reach the unsaved without a marketing budget. He challenged me and said, "Sergio, you have marketers in your church every week. Commission *them*. Have a BYOB service."

I wrote down BYOB and immediately I heard, "Bring Your Own Buddy."

Right away our church got to work on a campaign to invite five friends to a BYOB service. The name attracted people who would have never come to church otherwise. Additionally, it challenged the church to take ownership over the growth of God's house. We looked at our sanctuary and began to see every chair as an empty heart.

It dramatically changed the way the church looked at inviting our friends. We no longer just saw it as bringing our friends and family to hear a message or fill a service. It caused us to remember what it felt like to have an empty heart. Our services grew because our hearts grew. The church began to see soul winning as their responsibility every day.

The principles of one of my favorite stories in the Bible drive me to never forget that the greatest responsibility as a revolutionary is to love people back to life—the famous story of the Good Samaritan. To make the point that God loves everyone, especially outcasts, Jesus tells the story of a man who was beaten, stripped, and left for dead and the reject who saved his life:

> A certain man went down from Jerusalem to Jericho, and fell among thieves, who stripped him of his clothing, wounded him, and departed, leaving him half dead. Now by chance a certain priest came down that road. And when he saw him, he passed by on the other side. Likewise a Levite, when he arrived at the place, came and looked, and passed by on the other side. But a certain Samaritan, as he journeyed, came where he was. And when he saw him, he had compassion. So he went to him and bandaged his wounds, pouring on oil and wine; and he set him on his own animal, brought him to an inn, and took care of him. On the next day, when he departed, he took out two denarii, gave them to the innkeeper, and said to him, "Take care of him; and whatever more you spend, when I come again, I will repay you." (Luke 10:30–36)

God has used this story in my life to reveal five heart commitments that have kept my heart focused on rescuing others. Let's look at these heart commitments so that we can continue to bring this revolution to those around us.

◆ A heart commitment to never forget the pain of when we were brought back to life.

Every one of us has a story of when God rescued us. Many times He found us in the same condition as this man— broken, hurting, and alone. Remembering the emotions and pain of being rescued from situations that we could never rescue ourselves from allows us to relate to those who still need rescuing. Because Christ completely redeems us, restores us, and makes us whole, it can be easy to forget how desperate we were at one time. When we remember the pain we experienced before we were rescued—not with the purpose of wallowing in our sins, but to realize the depths of God's grace—we give God permission to send us the lost, the hurting, and the broken, because He knows we'll take care of them. He knows we won't walk away or ignore their pain. He knows we'll stand in the gap and be part of the answer. He knows that we will keep a humble heart before Him and others and not allow pride to get in the way of someone else's miracle.

He knows this because we remember what it felt like to be rescued.

◆ A heart commitment to make turning the hearts of others our business.

The moment our hearts turn, we receive a new vocation in life. We join God in the business of soul winning. Our primary business is to be an evangelist at work, at school, and at home. God partners with us to remind us we have been rescued to be more than spectators of other people's pain. We have been rescued to be liberators. The priest and the Levite were called and trained to liberate the broken, the destitute, and the hurting, yet their response was to walk around the problem instead of getting involved. You have been authorized by God to turn hearts, but it's up to you to use that authority. You're the answer to your community. You're the answer at your workplace. You're the answer at your schools. You are the answer. Making a heart decision to love people back to life will always challenge you to get personally involved with those you've been called to liberate.

> Rescue the perishing;
>   don't hesitate to step in and help.
> If you say, "Hey, that's none of my business,"
>   will that get you off the hook?
> Someone is watching you closely, you know—
> Someone not impressed with weak excuses.
> (Prov. 24:11 Message)

◆ **A heart commitment to be emotionally and spiritually moved with compassion by the hurt and pain of others.**

Compassion is the most powerful force on earth. It will cause you to love the unlovable and do the unthinkable. It will move you to carry the weight of others until you see them break through. The Samaritan was moved to care for a man he had never met to such a degree that he bandaged his wounds and cared for his needs as though the man were his own flesh and blood. His compassion and generosity were revealed when he was moved to do more than watch this man suffer.

Our hearts, filled with compassion, move us from *doing* church to *being* the church. When we arm ourselves with compassion, God trusts us with His most valuable commodity—souls.

◆ **A heart commitment to risk our reputation and leave our comfort zone.**

A heart to rescue others knows no limitations. There is no boundary that love and compassion won't cross to see the wounds of another healed. When the ache and cry of the hurting reaches into your heart, there is no perception, opinion, or cost that is too great to bring them to healing. The Good Samaritan could have walked away, but he risked being ridiculed, mocked, and punished because he couldn't ignore what he saw and what he felt. If he had hesitated and considered how others would perceive his actions before he stepped in, he most likely would have passed right by and kept walking. The reality is, a missed opportunity can mean a missed eternity. Everyone wants to go to heaven, but what are we doing to help take as many people with us? People who are hurting need more than just a passing glance. They need to know there are people who have been rescued who will risk it all to now rescue them. When we risk it all, the reward is precious hearts and lives turned back to God:

231

My dear friends, if you know people who have wandered off from God's truth, don't write them off. Go after them. Get them back and you will have rescued precious lives from destruction and prevented an epidemic of wandering away from God. (James 5:19–20 Message)

♦ **A heart commitment to use our resources to restore others back to life.**

Taking on Christ's heart for others is always costly. Loving people back to life will always challenge us to use our resources of time, money, and possessions to help those in need. The Samaritan used his oil, wine, and cloth to bandage the man's wounds. The coins he gave to the innkeeper were enough for two weeks of room and board. He even promised to come back and pay the difference if it cost more than that. There's no hint that he gave grudgingly at all. It overflowed from him.

When we freely give as the Samaritan did, our resources allow God to use every possible avenue and opportunity to reach the lost. Our resources tell God we are serious about taking care of people because every offering, every conversation, every generous act, and every selfless deed opens up the floodgates for healing and restoration.

One of the greatest lies prevalent in believers is that our resources don't matter in the kingdom of God. However, this story of the Good Samaritan demonstrates to us the value our resources have in the lives of those God longs to rescue. You need to know that your resources matter to God, because it matters in the lives of those who need it most. In fact, your sacrifice is so important to God that He says to you the same words the Samaritan said to the innkeeper. He will return to you, in abundance, anything you sow to rescue the lost. The Bible says whatever you release today goes into your future with the promise of a return far greater than you could ever imagine or expect:

And Jesus replied, "Let me assure you that no one has ever given up anything—home, brothers, sisters, mother, father, children, or property—for love of Me and to tell others the Good News, who won't be given back, a hundred times over, homes, brothers, sisters, mothers, children, and land." (Mark 10:29–30 TLB)

The truth is that we can't outgive God, because He was the One who paid the ultimate price to rescue the hurting, the broken, and the rejected. But join me today in declaring that you and I will do our part to be the answer for someone else. Together let's make these heart commitments to love people back to life and begin a revolution in this generation. Believe that you are the answer the world has been waiting for.

34

Compassion in Action

If Christ lives in us, controlling our personalities, we will leave glorious marks on the lives we touch. Not because of our lovely characters, but because of His.

—Eugenia Price, novelist and activist

Have you ever heard what sounds like direction from God and then thought, "There's no way this could be God"? This past Mother's Day, that was exactly my thought when I heard God say to me, "Sergio, I want you to give away a new car to a mom in need this Mother's Day." I remember thinking, "No way could God be telling me to do this. This is insane." We were already set in motion to give away over a thousand corsages to every mom on Sunday morning, just as we have done for the past five years. I pushed the idea out of my head but kept feeling it tug at my heart.

Less than two weeks before the big day, we began finalizing details at our weekly staff meeting for our plans for Mother's Day. Everything was prepared and every detail was set in place. But I knew I heard God's direction and He didn't tell me to give away corsages. He told me to give away a brand-new car.

As I sat in the staff meeting, I heard God's voice again speak to my heart, "Sergio, I want to help a mom. I want to give away a brand-new car to lighten a mom's load." I stopped the staff meeting and said, "We need to give away a car for Mother's Day."

My staff looked at me stunned for only a moment before they began to get excited about how to make this happen. In the next fifteen minutes, we planned, organized, and made preparations to hold an essay contest for kids to be able to write in why their mom deserved a car. All that was missing was a car. I packed up and headed off to the local dealerships to plead our case. I tried every dealership I could to get even a used car, but everyone's response was the same: "It's a nice idea, but you're crazy to try to give away a car in economic times like this." One guy actually told me, "What you want to do is impossible. There's no way you're going to be able to do it." But I wasn't going to let God be denied. We were in it to win it.

The following night at our midweek service, I stood before the church and told them what God had told us to do. Their response was phenomenal and overwhelming. One of the most beautiful things I've seen our church do over and over again throughout the years is give till it hurts. The love of Christ has captured their hearts, and they jump in to help whenever they see someone in need. Compassionate action is woven into the culture of our church. They don't sit back when they see a need. They choose instead to sow a seed to meet that need. And this Mother's Day was no exception.

Through the incredible generosity of our church, we were able to purchase a brand-new car with cash. There wasn't a dry eye in our church the night we read the winning essay of a mom whose daughter had been murdered just one year before, only a few days after Mother's Day. She was now raising her daughter's children and had no transportation to take her children and grandchildren to school, to the grocery store, to the doctors, or even to visit her daughter's gravesite. We wept together as she kept thanking us over and over again. It was a historic night for us as a church family, because the heartbeat of God echoed through her words and penetrated our hearts. His compassion had invaded the hearts of our church once again and, as a result, a family would never be the same.

Compassionate action is woven into the culture of our church.

When we allow our hearts to put compassion into action, we grow closer to Christ and our hearts become more like His. We come to the conviction that turning the hearts of others is our responsibility. Many times we look at people's situations that break our heart and we feel sympathy for them, but it's *empathy* that will move us from emotion to action. Sympathy will lead us to care from a distance, but it doesn't compel us to step in and make a difference. Empathy doesn't allow us to stand back and simply watch. It allows us to feel the pain and ache of a broken heart to such a degree that we can't help but respond. The Bible says we can't merely say we have love in our hearts for others. We must put it into action:

> Suppose someone sees a brother or sister in need and is able to help them. If he doesn't take pity on them, how can the love of God be in him? Dear children, don't just talk about love. Put your love into action. Then it will truly be love. (1 John 3:17–18 NIrV)

Years ago when God first placed the desire in my heart to start a church, I met with an old friend in Santa Barbara and shared with him my vision for the church. He looked at me and said, "Sergio, if you want to really help people, you need two things: a big heart and a big wallet. You can't really help people without both of them." After over a decade of pastoring Cornerstone Church, I've come to realize how true his words were.

It's vital that we stay connected to the emotional, spiritual, and material needs in people's lives by opening up our hearts to them. The love of God in action in our lives brings healing to someone else's.

One of the greatest tragedies is when a person forgets where God has brought them from and has lost sight of their mission in life to turn the hearts of others. I've known too many believers who spend all their time in a nice Christian community, going to nice Christian events, surrounded by nice Christian people. Unwittingly, they've created a spiritual country club.

To rescue the lost, there has to be a "whatever it takes, whatever it costs" attitude. My challenge to you today is to take on the "whatever it takes, whatever it costs" perspective when it comes to reaching out to those in need. A perspective that is committed to raise your voice for people who can't speak up for themselves—those who are addicted, abused, ailing, and afflicted.

It was this perspective that caused a revolution in our church's heart to start a ministry called Voice—the compassionate arm of Cornerstone that focuses on social justice and spiritual deliverance. This is how we as a church are able to answer the cry of our generation by reaching out to the homeless, to the community, and to those in need of a rehabilitation center. Our Restoration Ranch houses both men and women who are on their way to living a clean, sober, and changed life. Voice was birthed from a Scripture that challenged our church to truly put compassion into action:

> Speak up for the people who have no voice,
>   for the rights of all the down-and-outers.

Speak out for justice!
    Stand up for the poor and destitute! (Prov. 31:8–9
    Message)

If those who long to be rescued could speak up, what would it sound like? What would it look like? I believe it would look like the same demographic that caused Jesus to step out of heaven, carry the cross for our sins, and be crucified over 2,000 years ago. It would look like a generation hoping to figure out how to make their marriages work, how to raise their children, how to care for sick or elderly parents, how to jump-start a stalled career, how to get out from under the crushing weight of debt. A generation trying to make the pieces of their lives fit together, some for the first time, and some who are trying again and again. And all the while they're seeing the revolution in your life, wondering how they can find it for themselves.

Raise your voice for people who can't speak up for themselves.

When we take steps to care for those in need, God shares His heart with us and we begin to feel what He feels. Just like Him, we rejoice with those who rejoice, and our hearts break with those who are suffering. And we, broken but redeemed people, have the incredible privilege of representing the God of the universe to the people we meet. At every point that God uses us to spark a Heart Revolution in someone's life, we tap into the very heartbeat of God.

In an article written decades ago called "The Emotional Life of Our Lord," Dr. B. B. Warfield observed that the most common emotion in Jesus' life, identified by the Gospel writers, is compassion—more than all other emotions put together. Showing compassion allows us to draw on the very character of Jesus and become like Him. And as He captures our hearts, His love flows freely from us to others.

35

A Thirst for Justice

Today, see if you can stretch your heart and expand your love so that it touches not only those to whom you can give it easily, but also those who need it so much.

— Daphne Rose Kingma, author

As we grow closer to Christ and understand more of His heart and His purposes, we begin to see more and more how, in Him, grace and justice are beautifully intertwined. The prophet Isaiah tells us that when God saw the oppression of His people, "it displeased Him that there was no justice"(Isa. 59:15). All throughout Scripture we see that both the Father and Son had a thirst for justice.

When Jesus saw religious leaders prevent people from being healed, He got angry. When He walked into the Temple and saw that it had been turned into a den of thieves where people wanted to make money instead of worship the Father, He was furious. These acts of injustice angered Him and impelled

Him to act radically for justice. Today, He desires that we make the same radical impact on our generation when we see injustice take place.

The more we are in tune with God's heart, the more we will feel broken and angered at injustice, as Jesus did. Seeing a person who is the victim of injustice will produce the same kind of emotion in us as it did in Christ: righteous anger. Many people are afraid of anger, and find it difficult to think of anger—any anger—as being godly and good, but the kind Jesus modeled is not only right, it's necessary for those who follow in His footsteps. This anger, though, is categorically different from the kind of anger we see prevalent today. Righteous anger isn't out of control, and it's not self-absorbed. Anger at injustice is right and necessary, but only if it is shaped and balanced by the love of Christ. The prophet Micah described this blend:

The righteous anger Jesus modeled is not only right, it's necessary.

> And what does the LORD require of you?
> To act justly and to love mercy
> and to walk humbly with your God. (Micah 6:8 NIV)

Simplified, justice without mercy is like anger without purpose. It's mercy that tempers justice and propels us to take action against injustice. But don't miss the other necessary component in Micah's message. We won't be able to draw mercy or justice from our hearts unless we first humbly trust God to change us. The more you become humbled by God's love and forgiveness, the more you care about the people Jesus died to save. When you see them in trouble, you are quick to step in and help because you're living out the new nature that has developed as a result of your heart experiencing a revolution.

Our longing for justice is rooted in God's complete commitment to make justice reign on earth through the sacrifice of His Son. It's only at the feet of Jesus Christ that our thirst for justice is quenched. Justice isn't second place to God; it's second nature. It was His thirst for justice that moved the Father to send His only Son to rescue a lost and hurting people and restore the relationship between Him and all humankind. Justice flows from the heart of God and, through the Heart Revolution, we see it begin to flow out of us into our relationships.

Justice isn't second place to God; it's second nature.

I remember a family that came through the doors of our church, broken and hurting. Going to church was their last hope. In fact, divorce papers had already been filed and boxes were already packed. As they walked into the sanctuary, worship began to do what words couldn't. The presence of God began to break through years of hurt, and by the end of worship the entire family was weeping.

Years later the husband shared with me, "I don't know what happened. I was so angry when I came in, but something changed while I was standing there. I can't explain it. I just know that for the first time I felt like I was right with God, and instead of being angry at my wife, I just wanted to make it right with her too." Instead of wanting to repay offense for offense, they chose to make things right. This shift caused them to stay married and begin to work out issues that for too long had not been dealt with. It took tremendous courage to believe that justice for the wrongs they had committed had been satisfied on the cross. They were finally free from the vicious cycle of revenge.

Instead of excuses, they began to apologize. Instead of pointing fingers, they began to forgive. And instead of walking away, they chose to stick it out. Though it took time to heal the wounds of the past, this couple eventually overcame years of hurt, betrayal, and offense. The decision this couple made to "make things right" changed the direction of their marriage and brought healing to an entire family.

Over the years I've discovered that sometimes the reason we struggle to respond to injustice is simply because we don't yet fully grasp the price Jesus paid to forgive us. The Bible says that when we struggle to believe we are wholly and completely forgiven, it is difficult to extend God's love to others:

> Anyone who has been forgiven for only a little will show only a little love. (Luke 7:47 CEV)

But when our hearts become revolutionized by the depth of God's forgiveness and love, it changes us, like this couple, from the inside out.

Injustice is given free rein in our communities, in our homes, and in our hearts when disorder and imbalance run rampant. In the midst of disorder, His love, which is the light in our hearts, begins to dim. When we see people in need and don't respond, the light in our heart dims. When we use harsh words with a spouse or child, the light in our home dims. And when we lie to one another or avoid talking about the issues and conflicts that threaten our relationships, it dims even more. But Jesus said,

> I am the world's Light. No one who follows me stumbles around in the darkness. I provide plenty of light to live in. (John 8:12 Message)

Living out a conviction of truth, righteousness, and grace brings the light of justice to our relationships, our homes, and our personal lives. Justice is found in the extension of our heart and hands toward those in need, and in our commitment to spend time at home interacting with our kids. In practical terms, justice can be as simple as a decision to start loving people regardless of their condition, or to remove hurtful words from our relational vocabulary, or to choose to be financially obedient in our tithe. Most times justice is found in the small ways we respond to the world around us, yet its impact is far from small.

Begin today to see your role in the Heart Revolution as one who has been commissioned by the Justifier to bring justice to an unjust world.

36

Evangelism:
Reaching the Lost at All Cost

> May God deliver us from self-righteous judging
> and make us, instead, merciful carriers of Christ's
> salvation and freedom everywhere we go.
>
> —Pastor Jim Cymbala

Every year thousands of families join us for our annual Easter egg hunt outreach, and every year more and more kids come ready to fill their baskets and bags with eggs. It's a wonderful time for us as a church and as a community—one we look forward to every year. The fields are covered with hundreds and hundreds of parents and children waiting for their opportunity to run and grab as many eggs as possible.

I'll never forget the year our greatest fear happened. A mother came up to one of our leaders frantically screaming, "I can't find my son! I lost my son!"

It was as if time stood still for a few moments as her words registered in our minds. I remember looking out over the field and seeing what seemed like thousands and thousands of kids, thinking, "How are we going to find her son with all these kids?"

Jesus came here on a search and rescue mission.

Immediately our team jumped into action, and within minutes her son was returned to her, his mouth full of candy, oblivious to the panic his mother had gone through. Through tears of relief, this mother began to tell everyone, "I found him! He's OK!"

I've thought about that mother many times over the years as I stood before our church and made the plea for people to turn their heart to Jesus Christ. I remember the desperation in her voice as she cried out for someone to help her find her lost son. I imagine it's the same desperation a mother or father feels when they're begging for God to find their son or daughter who is lost to an addiction, or the desperation of a spouse crying out to Jesus for their spouse who has gone astray. It's the same desperation of a teenager reaching out to the Savior for a parent who has abandoned them.

When someone you love is lost, all you're concerned about is finding them. The heart of the Father is moved in the exact same way toward those who are lost. In fact, the Bible says Jesus came here on a search and rescue mission:

> For the Son of Man came to seek and save those who are lost. (Luke 19:10 NLT)

Everything Jesus did was with the purpose of rescuing the lost, because He was aware that eternal destinies were at stake. All that He did during His time on earth was shaped and motivated by His reality of heaven. When you become convinced, as Jesus was, that lost people will miss out on the opportunity of heaven, you're far more willing to pay any cost to reach them with the message of God's forgiveness. You will gladly pay the physical, financial, or relational cost of reaching the lost when the prospect of ensuring their eternity with Him is in the balance. When heaven is at stake, the lines that separate communities become obscure, and you don't mind going where those who are lost live, whether it be the suburbs or the 'hood, to bring them the hope of eternity.

In one of His parables, Jesus told a story of a banquet which gives us a glimpse of the Father's heart for rescuing the lost. A man threw an elaborate banquet and sent his servant to invite people to come. The master in the story is a type, a shadow, of God, and the banquet is the celebration for people who enter His kingdom. When the guests gave excuses for their absence, the master told the servant, "Go out quickly into the streets and lanes of the city, and bring in here the poor and the maimed and the lame and the blind" (Luke 14:21). The servant immediately reported that he had already done that, but there was still room for more. The master then commanded him, "Go out into the highways and hedges, and compel them to come in, that my house may be filled" (Luke 14:23).

Notice the attitude of the master. He wasn't content to settle for excuses. He was insistent the servant do whatever it took to fill his house. He instructed the servant to "compel" people to come. The word "compel" means to use force, in this case, to literally drag people back to the banquet.

Today, Jesus is saying the same thing to you. Compel your friends, family, and loved ones to come to His house so that it may be filled. Compel them by using whatever means necessary and bring them to the feet of Jesus.

To most, this concept is revolutionary, but let me remind you of the mother who dragged people she had never met to help her find her lost son. In this context it doesn't seem so ridiculous. The idea of never seeing her son again caused her to forget about being socially acceptable or politically correct. Again, all she thought of was finding her son.

In the same way, we must view the possibility of not seeing our family and friends in eternity as our launching pad to do whatever it takes to fill heaven. If one attempt fails, try something else. If one way of communicating the message of hope doesn't make an impact, try a different method. Don't give up when you feel resistance to your first invitation. Ask again, and again, and again.

Don't give up when you feel resistance to your first invitation.

Sometimes the very thing that will start the Heart Revolution within a person is knowing that someone wouldn't give up on them. They just don't know how to communicate to you their need to be asked again. On countless occasions in our services during an altar call, I have asked the church to turn to the person sitting next to them and ask them if they need to go up to the altar and ask Jesus into their heart. There have been times when the Holy Spirit has compelled me to have them ask not once, not twice, but three times because their eternity is on the line. And time and time again, people who wouldn't respond the first or second time will step out of their seat and walk to the front with tears in their eyes when they're asked a third time.

When it comes to filling God's house, keep asking. Even if you feel uncomfortable or nervous, keep asking. Even if you don't have all the right answers, keep asking. You never know if all they need is just one more invitation. They may be one question away from heaven.

Years ago I did a funeral for a gang member who had been murdered. I watched as the church filled up with young men and women who were locked into a life they couldn't escape. My heart broke for the pain I saw in their eyes. They weren't just mourning the life of a friend, brother, son, and homie. They were mourning their own life as well, as the reality of their humanity was in front of them. They weren't delusional about the fact that life and death were constantly in front of them. One by one they walked in knowing that it could have been any one of them in the casket that night.

The Holy Spirit began to speak to me, "Sergio, you can reach them. Their hearts are open for change. Ask them if they'll let Me come into their hearts."

It was the first time I had ever heard the prompting of the Holy Spirit to do an altar call at a funeral, but it wasn't the last. At the end of the funeral, I looked out into the seats filled with gangbangers and said, "I may never see you again, so I need to ask you one of the most important questions you've ever been asked. More important than the question of where you're from or what gang you belong to. I need to ask you, if you were to die tomorrow, would you wake up in heaven or hell? If you're not sure, I want to give you the opportunity to get right with God no matter what you've done and know without a shadow of a doubt that you'd wake up in heaven."

In the seconds that followed, I waited, unsure of what would happen next. Slowly hands began to rise all over the room until almost every hand was lifted for salvation.

Hundreds gave their lives to Christ that night. After that funeral, I went home in awe of what God had done in the hearts and lives of those who most people would call unreachable.

Less than a week later, one of those young men who had given his life to Jesus was murdered. His family shared with me the change in this young man's heart since he had received salvation and of his desire to walk away from the gang life forever. Their only peace was knowing that, without a shadow of a doubt, the next thing their son saw after being shot was the beauty of heaven.

When we really believe that eternity is at stake, we are compelled like the servant in Jesus' story to do whatever it takes to convince those who are lost to turn their heart to Him.

God wants you and me to go on a search and rescue for the lost so that heaven will be filled. The very heartbeat of heaven longs to rescue unsaved people. In your life, there are people God wants you to compel to His house with the message of hope. All you need to do is ask them the most important question of their life.

Whose heart will you turn for Christ today? Heaven is waiting.

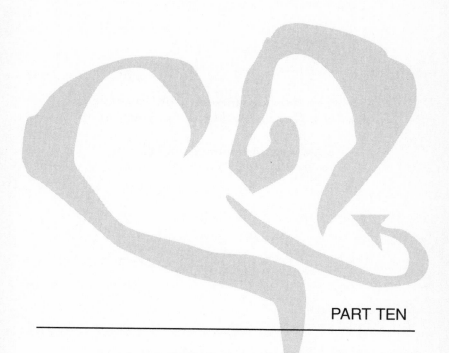

GETTING FIRED UP ABOUT YOUR FUTURE

Watch a special video message from Pastor Sergio
Part Ten: Getting Fired Up about Your Future

www.sergiodelamora.com/heartrev

37

Finding Your Place
in the Revolution

Passivity is not a valid response. We must become
active agents, forging the kind of response that is
spiritually and relationally authentic.

—Richard Swenson, author and educator

When I first felt God leading me to start a church in
San Diego, I was sure that He wanted the church
to attract people from the wealthy suburbs. After
all, I had lived in Santa Barbara, one of the most beautiful
and prosperous communities in the country. I naturally as-
sumed God wanted our new church to be a mirror of that
city. So when God placed our church in a high school in a
middle-class community, I wasn't sure what He was doing.
But I never stopped being obedient—even when He told us
to move from that middle-class community and buy a nine-

plex theater in National City, which was known as crime infested and impoverished. In those early days of the church, though I was obedient, I was still discovering my place in the revolution.

One day as I was asking God for direction, clarity, and wisdom, He spoke to me. "Sergio, stop being the pastor *you want to be*, and start being the pastor *the community needs you to be*." I knew exactly what He meant. For me to become the pastor God wanted me to be, and for our church to be what God intended, I had to revolutionize my heart again. It wasn't about what I wanted or even envisioned for the church. It was about fulfilling the mandate on the church to turn the hearts of youths and families back to God and back to each other. And when I did, the rest, as they say, is history. Even to this day, many years later, God has continued to pour out His unimaginable favor on us at Cornerstone, and we've had the privilege of seeing miraculous salvations, supernatural growth, and phenomenal transformation in the hearts of our church and community.

You are in a fight for the hearts of people in your family and community.

As you grow from spiritual infancy to adolescence, you may be tempted to think you've arrived and won't need any more heart surgery. But every one of us will continue to need God's surgical touch until we see Him face-to-face. At every point, our response is like the soldier who replies to orders, "Sir, I'm yours. Put me in wherever you want me to be." Just like a soldier, as a revolutionary, you are in a fight for the hearts of people in your family and community every day. But you aren't fighting alone. You're in God's army, united with a band of people who are connected in spirit and intent on one purpose—to turn more hearts back to Him.

Every family, every church, and every organization must go through three stages: family stage, team stage, and army stage. In the family stage, it's all about "whosoever." Whoever can step in to fill the need will be the one who fills the need. It's not about talent, gifting, abilities, or even if that person fits right. It's just about getting the needs met. At this stage you'll let someone operate in a position *knowing* they are the wrong person for the job, but it's whoever will step up and get it done. But you can only function in the family stage for so long before you need to transition to the team stage.

In the team stage, you start to discover the God-potential in each person, and you begin to place them where they best fit for the benefit of the entire team. The transition from family to team can be the most difficult for a family, church, or organization, because there now needs to be a shift from decisions based on *relationship* to decisions based on *calling* or *vocation*. This transition, more than any other, is the transition when more people become offended, angry, and frustrated. But without this critical transition, you won't be able to advance to the army stage. Every family, every church, and every organization should strive to become an army, because in the army stage you begin to function with the same strength as that of our armed forces. Though individual bravery is crucial, the entire army must work in tandem to achieve revolutionary results.

Armies function effectively with a clear sense of order, direction, and purpose. When they fight as a mob, victory eludes them, but when they obey the directions of their commander and follow the example of their leaders, they can accomplish revolutionary things. In today's mobile warfare, commanders call on the skills and resources of infantry, artillery, navy, and air power, all coordinated by a network of communications specialists. The potency of the armed forces is not found in their individual strength, but rather in their coordinated efforts.

It's time to find your place in the revolution. Maybe you've been in the family stage but you sense God's hand leading you to now become a team. Or maybe you've been training in the team stage and now it's time to join the revolution as a well-built army. Wherever you find yourself today, it's time to find your place in the revolution and discover more and more of the wonderful and amazing plans God has for your life. This discovery is waiting for you when you get involved in your local church. The local church is the anointed and appointed place that unlocks your breakthrough. God never meant for any of us to serve Him on our own. We are part of His body, interconnected and interdependent. I realize many people have suffered some of the most

God wants to revolutionize how you view His church!

painful hurts in churches, but just as God has revolutionized other areas of your life, He wants to now revolutionize how you view His bride, His church. When you are united with His Beloved, there's nothing like it on earth. You find people with similar joys and hurts, a similar vision for making a difference, and a similar passion for Christ. This heart connection with other believers keeps your life pumping with passion to live, love, and lead from your heart every day.

Many people have told me over the years, "I don't have any problem turning my heart, but I don't need to go to a church to do it." I always tell them being a believer who isn't connected to a local church is like saying you're a professional football player who doesn't play for a team. The reality is, you can't win the Super Bowl unless you're part of a team. Taking your place in the house of God goes beyond the confines of just "going to church." It stretches into who you are. You are the church. When you turn your heart, you are Christ's body, a tangible representation of Him to the people around you every day.

Paul describes our impact on the church as we each take our place:

He makes the whole body fit together perfectly. As each part does its own special work, it helps the other parts grow, so that the whole body is healthy and growing and full of love. (Eph. 4:16 NLT)

The church can only function well if we are connected to each other through loving, honest, supportive relationships. When you take your place, you become more than someone who just goes to church—you *are* the church.

In your community, every person behind every door is a mission field. In God's sovereignty, He has strategically placed you near people who need to hear the message of Christ's forgiveness. When you take your place in the revolution, you realize that every relationship, whether distant or close, matters for eternity. By taking your place in the Heart Revolution, you encourage others by your example. As they watch you, they feel encouraged to trust God and take their place in the revolution as well. Collectively, when we take our place, we unleash the power of God to turn more hearts and change more lives. Our strength lies in our ability to rise up in unison and answer the cry of the world. You are the answer. You're a carrier of God's Spirit, a revolutionary set apart to do His will. Your home, your church, and your community need you to step into your destiny.

Collectively, we unleash the power of God to turn hearts.

Josiah was eight years old when God challenged him to take his place as king (2 Kings 22:1). He had watched his father refuse to take his place, sabotage his destiny, and then be murdered by his own officials. Josiah pursued the promise of his destiny and followed God's direction, choosing not to repeat the pain of his family history. When he was faced with the sins of his ancestors, instead of making excuses, he took responsibility, repented, and raised a new standard of righteousness in his generation. As a result, the Bible records these profound words about this young man:

> Never before had there been a king like Josiah, who turned to the LORD with all his heart and soul and strength, obeying all the laws of Moses. And there has never been a king like him since. (2 Kings 23:25 NLT)

Josiah took a stand for righteousness, purity, and obedience in his generation, and God declared him a revolutionary unlike any before or after him. He took his place, even though he didn't see it modeled in the life of his father. His relationship with God revolutionized not only his life, but also the lives of all those after him. I believe this generation is the Josiah generation, called to take its place, raise a new standard of righteousness, and make a mark in history that is defined by revolutionary hearts for Jesus Christ.

When you know you've been called for greater purposes and you take a step into your destiny, nothing will stop you, not even death. At the moment of His betrayal, the Bible says Jesus didn't step back; He stepped forward to take His place in the revolution:

> Jesus fully realized all that was going to happen to him, so he stepped forward to meet them. (John 18:4 NLT)

Nothing that was waiting for Him on the other side of that step was enough to stop Him from taking His place. In the same way, there must be a determination and tenacity in you to step forward into your destiny. You just need to take that first step into finding your place as a revolutionary.

Step out today at home, at work, at your local church, at your school campus, and at your local community center. Take a revolutionary first step toward turning the hearts of others, and you'll discover your place in the revolution.

38

Quitting Isn't an Option

> Obstacles don't have to stop you. If you run into a
> wall, don't turn around and give up. Figure out how
> to climb it, go through it, or work around it.
>
> —Michael Jordan

It's inevitable. You're moving along, you're pressing in, you're making a difference, and then all of a sudden, something happens and you consider walking away. You're not alone. There comes a point in every revolutionary's life when quitting becomes a tempting option. It's not that you want to walk away and quit, because you don't. But life can come at you hard with a disappointment or discouragement that shakes your foundation, and you find yourself wondering if you're really on the right track or really doing the right thing in life. It's at that moment when all of us feel tempted to give up and give in.

The Heart Revolution is the greatest adventure of our lives, but in all true adventures, we face dangers, risks, and hardships. Even Jesus was tempted to quit, but He didn't because He knew what was at stake. He had preached the Good News all over the Promised Land. Everywhere He went, He healed the sick, raised the dead, cast out demons, gave sight to the blind, and taught God's truth to anyone who would listen. On the night before He took all the sins of the world on His shoulders, He realized the excruciating pain and the enormous cost He was going to pay (Matt. 26:39–44). Three times He prayed, "Father, let this cup pass," but He coupled that request with humble submission, "Not My will, but Yours." The next day, He endured the kind of pain none of us could ever experience. Because He didn't quit, we have life. As you understand how much Jesus endured for you, yet didn't quit, you'll find the strength to not quit.

On a few occasions when I've been discouraged, I've looked at Georgina and wondered if it's worth it to pour out our lives day after day, week after week. But as I keep pressing in and pushing through, I realize these moments don't last. When I step back and remember all God has done, I can't quit. I can't walk away because of a momentary setback. He reminds me that I am predestined to finish strong, and that knowledge puts purpose back into my heart. It's the same reminder Paul wrote about:

> Since future victory is sure, be strong and steady, always abounding in the Lord's work, for you know that nothing you do for the Lord is ever wasted. (1 Cor. 15:58 TLB)

Many times, we get discouraged and think about quitting when we find ourselves in the battle between "doing" versus "being." It's the moment when you're doing and doing at home, at work, and at church but you're losing your excitement and purpose. You have motion but no traction. You feel like your wheels are spinning but you're not making progress.

For many of us, this is the moment when you question the value and worth of continuing on. "Doing" isn't the basis of any relationship, but especially not one with God. His invitation to you wasn't so that you would be a slave to tasks. His invitation was for you to become His own child:

> Now you are no longer a slave but God's own child. And since you are his child, God has made you his heir. (Gal. 4:7 NLT)

When you go through life "doing" instead of "becoming," oftentimes you end up feeling inadequate, exhausted, and disappointed. You'll wrestle at God's prompting to do something because you'll only see the work, not the rewards. The reality is, "doing" doesn't guarantee you'll "become." Become what? Become confident and empowered in your relationship with Him. But choosing the pathway of "being" allows you to discover the joy, exhilaration, and the reward of fulfilling His work on earth. And when you're tempted to walk away, you'll stand in your relationship as a son or daughter and realize that nothing you ever do could separate you from Him.

We find ourselves in the battle between "doing" versus "being."

Years ago, a couple in our church went through one of the most painful experiences a couple can endure. They had been serving faithfully, growing in God and in their call. They were prominent leaders in our church; their testimony was an example and model for many. They were one of the first couples to be married in our church and were now expecting their first child.

As the weeks progressed into months, they excitedly and joyfully awaited the arrival of their new baby girl, Faith. But then, without any warning, they lost the baby. It was heart-wrenching and devastating for them, as well as for our entire church family. That night I went to the hospital, heartbroken for this beloved family, and sat in the lobby and had a conversation I will never forget with this man I had come to love and respect as my own son. I listened as he tearfully poured out his heart to me that he wasn't going to let his family quit on God, on each other, and on the hope that they would try again.

"Pastor, quitting is not an option for us." He just kept telling me over and over again, "Pastor, we can't quit. Quitting is not an option for us." I can't begin to put into words all that I felt sitting there listening to the relentless faith of this man. All I knew was somewhere in that conversation it was like I heard God whisper, "He needs to preach this coming weekend, Sergio."

I pushed it out of my mind, thinking it was absurd, but God's subtle prompting stayed with me. As I stood up, hugged him for a long time, and got ready to leave, it was stronger than ever.

I looked him in the eyes and said, "I know it sounds crazy, but I think you're supposed to preach this Sunday." He looked back into my eyes and nodded in stunned silence. He had never preached before, but the Holy Spirit wasn't talking only to me in the hospital lobby that night. He had felt the same prompting. That weekend, just days after his daughter went to heaven, he preached the first message of his life, entitled "Quitting Isn't an Option!" Years later, he shared with me that the moment he stepped onto that stage, his title went from mere words to rock-solid heart conviction. Today, this couple has two daughters, one son, and one little angel in heaven named Faith, who watches over them all.

Jesus never promised an easy life, but over and over again He assures you throughout Scripture that He will never leave you nor forsake you. The enemy will try to plant excuses in your mind to get you off track. If this father had listened to those lies, he would've found a dozen reasons why continuing to follow Christ made no sense at all. But instead he stood on truth and decided that, in actuality, it was *not* following God that made no sense. Jesus is the Creator of all, and He knows how your life is supposed to work. He is present with you at all times, so nothing is a surprise to Him. He holds all the power of the universe in His hands. Nothing you face is beyond His power to work miracles, but often, the miracle He wants to display for the world is to produce patience, obedience, and faithfulness in the hearts of His people.

God orchestrates His purposes in His way on His timetable.

We are real people who live in a real world, a world that at times is full of disappointments and heartache, but our God is powerful. He has proven that He has the power to change lives, and He's not finished with any of us yet. The world may try to convince you that He doesn't care, or that His power is limited, or that He's not even there at all—but those are lies. God's timing may be different than you'd like, but He orchestrates His purposes in His way on His timetable. And His purposes are always good. Nothing is impossible for God.

We all have days when we feel weak, discouraged, and disheartened, but how you handle these days says more about your character than you think. Today if you're tempted to quit, I encourage you to strengthen your heart by focusing on the love and power of Christ, His example of faithfulness, and the vision He has called you to accomplish. Let King David's own words remind you that, though you may feel knocked down, you are not knocked out.

I'm the anointed king. But today I'm weak. (2 Sam. 3:39 NIrV)

Even in your moments of weakness, you are still chosen and anointed to keep going. Press in to press through today. No matter what you feel, or what you're facing, you can keep going because Christ kept going. Because of who He is in your life, quitting will never be an option for you again.

39

Raising a Generation of Revolutionaries

The young do not know enough to be prudent, and therefore they attempt the impossible—and achieve it, generation after generation.

—Pearl S. Buck

No revolution overthrows a current system of belief or mentality without first establishing a new standard and precedence. It's not enough to rise up, revolt, and rebel. Every revolution must be defined by a purpose, a distinct vision. The Heart Revolution was birthed from God's heart not only to overthrow but, more importantly, to establish. We have been called as revolutionaries to establish a new standard of purity, righteousness, forgiveness, and obedience. But remember that it's the next generation that will build off that foundation. Our job is to set up the next generation so this movement of God's heart continues not just into their lives but also into every generation after them. They need to know, just like the disciples did, that they have been called for greater things. Jesus said,

> Most assuredly, I say to you, he who believes in Me, the works that I do he will do also; and greater works than these he will do. (John 14:12)

The heart decisions and choices you make today reach far beyond the present to revolutionize not only your future, but the future of all those connected to you. You are a revolutionary who has answered the call to revolutionize the next generation for Christ.

One of the most reflective questions we must now begin to answer is "What will happen to the next generation?" The next generation isn't like our generation. It's been shaped and formed by influential leaders, historical events, and pandemic trends

Our job is to set up the next generation so this movement of God's heart continues.

unlike any other generation before it. It's a sight-and-sound generation driven by social media, digital technologies, and political ventures that supersede anything we've ever seen before. And the one who can push past the images they see on their phones, computers, and other electronics to strike the chord and make them feel, think, sing, dance, and cry will be the one who holds their heart. There is only One who will penetrate the heart of the next generation with authenticity and legitimacy. That One is the revolutionary, Jesus Christ.

To raise revolutionaries that will follow after the One, we must be dedicated to understand what inspires them, what frustrates them, and what breaks their heart. Many of them have experienced the heartache of divorced parents, strained family relationships, and shattered friendships. They've known friends and peers who have tried to commit suicide, and some who have succeeded. They've witnessed crimes and violence to the point that they've become numb to it. They've been raised on broken families, broken homes, broken governments, and broken promises. The only way to reach this generation is to possess and exemplify the one thing it longs for—commitment. There is a craving for a genuine commitment to rebuild the foundation of all that the next generation has seen torn down. It's a commitment like Paul spoke about when he used his life as an example to the Corinthians:

> Every bit of my commitment is for the purpose of building you up, after all, not tearing you down. (2 Cor. 10:8 Message)

One of the main questions every pastor asks is, "How do I raise future leaders?"

As our church was growing, I began to feel the challenge to raise future leaders, but not just leaders who could maintain the work. I felt God challenge me to raise leaders who could take the church into the future. This triggered a desire to do a new conference dedicated to raise the next generation. We call it "The Uprising."

God kept telling us to do more than just host a conference for the next generation. He kept telling us these three words: "Share the stage." Over and over again we kept hearing God say the same thing: "Share the stage."

Nothing transmits our mission and passion for a revolution to the next generation like giving them the opportunity to express who they are on the inside. We have to be willing to share our stage with them, not just literally but spiritually and relationally as well. They need to know they can release what is brewing inside of them so that they can learn to refine and shape it for their future. Nothing empowers the next generation more than giving them a platform to use their gifts and talents.

So we decided to do something we had never seen before. We decided to hold a Preach-off Competition. It was an opportunity for students to get up for two minutes and preach the gospel of Jesus Christ. They chose a text and explained the what, why, and how to an audience of their peers and a panel of judges. We opened up the stage to a group of young adults, most of whom had never been given the opportunity to stand center stage with the lights, sound, and video, and let the anointing to preach come forth. With their peers roaring in the audience, their confidence soared.

It's said that, in the animal kingdom, the greatest hunters are those that have smelled the scent of blood from their first kill. Once they smelled that scent from their first kill, they would never forget that scent. It would propel them to crave it for the rest of their life. Getting these students on the stage was like having them smell that first scent of purpose. We believe they will never go back now that they had a glimpse of their future. For some, that was all the confirmation they needed to keep pursuing their calling.

You can't give away something that you don't first possess.

This generation, our generation, is desperate to make a commitment to help the next generation live out their call. There is a hunger in them to right the wrongs, to stand for those who have fallen, to rebuild what has been broken down, and to display an unquestionable commitment to capture the heart of the next generation. We have a responsibility to re-inspire them to follow Christ by modeling an example marked by truth and faithfulness. They will learn to love God with all their hearts, value the things God values, and make choices each day to follow Him in their relationships and desires from watching you and me set the example. That's why this Heart Revolution is so powerful. You can't give away something that you don't first possess. Before it can overflow from you, it must first overtake you.

Most of what we are dealing with today in our families is the result of what the previous generation could not conquer. Poor decisions of past generations can be felt for years, but in the same way, right decisions and right commitments can turn history around for all future generations. In the Bible, Hezekiah took his place as king in a generation that had turned away from God. He saw the devastating effects the past decisions of their ancestors had on their families, and he chose to stand up and lead the revolution:

> In the first month of the first year of his reign, Hezekiah, having first repaired the doors of The Temple of GOD, threw them open to the public. He assembled the priests . . . and said, . . . "Our ancestors went wrong and lived badly before GOD—they discarded him, turned away . . . and walked off. . . . This is why our ancestors were killed, and this is why our wives and sons and daughters were taken prisoner and made slaves. I have decided to make a covenant with the GOD of Israel and turn history around." (2 Chron. 29:3, 6, 9–10 Message)

God is challenging you to make the same commitment today. The next generation doesn't have to live as slaves because of the mistakes of their parents, grandparents, or great-grandparents. You can take a stand today to change everything. You can choose to rewrite history for the next generation by what you do today. Just because the last generation didn't go to college doesn't mean you won't get your master's. Just because they ended up in divorce doesn't mean your marriage won't last. And just because they didn't serve God doesn't mean that you won't serve Him wholeheartedly for the rest of your life.

I'm telling you today, you didn't just press through this *Heart Revolution* journey to not see the change you prayed for come to pass in the lives of your children and your children's children. Decide to make a commitment to stand against the generational curses and strongholds that have held your family back, just as King Hezekiah did. And the hope and future of the next generation will stand because of it.

Generational changes happen not only through bold decisions such as Hezekiah's, but also through a powerful combination of God's Word, the power of the Holy Spirit, and the prayers of those who will stand in the gap for the next generation of revolutionaries. Your prayers don't go unnoticed, unheard, or unanswered. God has not called you "parent," "pastor," or "youth leader" without a purpose. Your prayers are more powerful than you think. They impact the next generation in both the seen and unseen world. Your example to pray earnestly for the next generation demonstrates to them your commitment to see them succeed. And in the spiritual realm, when you pray for them, you radically protect the destiny and calling over their lives. As God works deeply in them and you cover their lives in prayer, He gives them fresh revelation on how their lives count for eternity, and they realize they have to depend on Him to make a difference in the world.

> **Your prayers impact the next generation in both the seen and unseen world.**

What then do we pray for when we pray for the next generation? Paul's prayers for people in the churches where he modeled love and life give us a sound example to follow. In his letter to the Colossians, he told them,

> We have been asking God to fill you with the knowledge of what he wants. We pray that he will give you spiritual wisdom and understanding. We pray that you will lead a life that is worthy of the Lord. We pray that you will please him in every way. So we want you to bear fruit in every good thing you do. We want you to grow to know God better. We want you to be very strong, in keeping with his glorious power. We want you to be patient. Never give up. (1:9–11 NIrV)

Just imagine for a moment what our churches, our society, and our nation would look like when parents, pastors, and youth leaders begin to pray like Paul. Words like "We pray that you will lead a life that is worthy of the Lord" are revolutionary in our culture today. But they need to know that you will cover them, protect them, believe in them, encourage them, and stand in the gap for them.

Every child, every teenager, and every twentysomething in your world is the hope of the future. These next-generation leaders will be marked by their passion to live, love, and lead from their hearts. They will pass on this Heart Revolution long after we have fulfilled our own call. They are revolutionaries in their own right, and it's our responsibility, privilege, and mission to give them the tools necessary for them to succeed in every area of their lives. The Bible commands them to obey and honor their parents, but it doesn't just stop there. It continues with these words to the parents as well:

> Don't keep on scolding and nagging your children, making them angry and resentful. Rather, bring them up with the loving discipline the Lord himself approves, with suggestions and godly advice. (Eph. 6:4 TLB)

Does this mean you don't discipline or correct them when they're on the wrong course? Absolutely not. No, it means that as you make a commitment to raise the next generation in your home, in your church, and in the community, you never lose sight of the fact that you are raising up a true *revolutionary*, someone who has been called to overthrow the present standard or mindset by establishing the supremacy of a new precedence that causes dramatic change.

They are the future, but they need you now. They need your commitments, your love, and your faith every day. Your commitment today cleanses their generation and gives them room to become who God has called them to be. If you've struggled to connect to the next generation, ask God to enlarge your vision for them so that you may see them as He sees them.

Just as the Father called His Son His Beloved, so does He call our sons and daughters. They are His beloved generation, set apart to do amazing things for Him. Partner with Him today to raise a generation that will change the world forever.

40

If Not You, Then Who?

If not you, then who? If not now, then when?

—Hillel

You are almost to the finish line of this journey called the Heart Revolution and with the prize of completion comes genuine transformation. You're not the same person you were when you began this journey. You've pushed through, endured, and overcome. For the last month, you have gained insight, perspective, and vision for your future to live, lead, and love with purpose. But the Heart Revolution isn't meant to end with the last page. It is meant to last a lifetime. Once you close this book for the last time, it will be the condition and quality of your heart that keeps the revolution alive inside you. As you reflect on the past forty days, I want to ask you three final questions:

- If not you, then who?
- If not here, then where?
- If not now, then when?

Throughout history, sometimes an obscure, unassuming person steps up and makes a tremendous difference in the lives of a family, a city, or a nation. King Solomon's words confirm to us that the condition of our birth doesn't necessarily determine our future:

> Even if you were not born into the royal family and have been a prisoner and poor, you can still be king. (Eccles. 4:14 CEV)

People who step up, take their place in the Heart Revolution, and change the world aren't any different from you or me. They have the same desires and fears, but they've made a choice to make their lives count. They're convinced of three crucial truths:

- They have a cause that's worth living for and dying for.
- They have passed the point of no return.
- They are convinced that it all starts with them.

Esther didn't see herself as a heroine. Through some odd circumstances, this beautiful young Jewish woman found herself the Queen of Persia. But Haman, one of the king's nobles, hated the Jews and plotted to kill them all by convincing the king to issue a decree to kill every Jew. At that pivotal moment in the history of God's people, Esther's cousin Mordecai realized that God had put Esther in the strategic position as the queen to rescue their people. He asked her to risk her life by going to the king without being invited so she could ask him to change his edict to kill the Jews. When she hesitated, Mordecai told her,

The Heart Revolution isn't meant to end with the last page.

Do not think in your heart that you will escape in the king's palace any more than all the other Jews. For if you remain completely silent at this time, relief and deliverance will arise for the Jews from another place, but you and your father's house will perish. Yet who knows whether you have come to the kingdom for such a time as this? (Esther 4:13–14)

God had put Esther at that place at a crucial moment in history. When she realized this and understood what was at stake, she obeyed. She risked it all to rescue her people.

I believe God has put each of us in a particular place with particular people at a particular time in history for the same reason: to rescue, restore, and revolutionize.

For many of you, the reality that God has chosen this moment in history to use you as a revolutionary is unbelievable, incomprehensible, and inconceivable. But through this Heart Revolution, you have already begun to believe in the unbelievable. Why stop now? You believe in God, you believe in heaven, you believe that He has turned your heart and that your sins are forgiven. Why stop there? Continue to believe in the unbelievable. As you keep walking out the keys and principles of the Heart Revolution, I challenge you to begin to welcome things to come into your life that seem too good to be true. His favor, His goodness, and His forgiveness are not just topics you've read about in the last forty days. They are living truths, active beliefs, and personal heart commitments that attract His unbelievable blessings for the entirety of your life.

God has chosen this moment in history to use you as a revolutionary.

These upcoming weeks aren't the time to pull back from His Word, His presence, and His purposes. I want to challenge you not to close this book, put it on the shelf, and walk away. As you continue to walk out the spiritual heart habits of daily spending time reading His Word and staying in constant communication with Him through prayer, keep this book with you and reflect on what you've experienced.

Remember, this revolution isn't just something you *did*—it's who you *are*.

At one point in Jesus' ministry, two men said they would follow Him, but only on their terms. They both stated conditions for their obedience. Luke tells us the first man's response to Jesus' invitation was,

> "Lord, let me first go and bury my father.". . .
> And another also said, "Lord, I will follow You, but let me first go and bid them farewell who are at my house."
> But Jesus said to him, "No one, having put his hand to the plow, and looking back, is fit for the kingdom of God." (Luke 9:59–62)

Jesus' words may sound harsh, but as always, He was dealing with their hearts, not their excuses.

When you step out in faith and live this revolution from the inside out every single day, you may be tempted to find excuses. You may be afraid of the future, but stay confident in God because you've seen His faithfulness at work in the past. You may be unsure of how to take all that you've learned and apply it to your everyday life, but stay connected to the truths He's deposited into your heart and pray for His wisdom and direction. Or you may feel worried about making mistakes and ending up on the wrong track, but stay full of faith that the One who rescued you before will rescue you again and again if necessary.

Over the past weeks, you have conquered more than you ever imagined and overcome more than you ever dreamed. But there is one last venture that you must face in order to help you stay on the right track. Take a moment and reflect on the *one area* of your life that you have carried with you since the onset of this book that you're now ready to let go of. Maybe it's an unfulfilled dream that keeps gnawing at your heart. Or maybe it's a relationship that you've carried with you since page 1 that God has been telling you to release. Maybe it's an email you never sent or a letter you never wrote. Maybe it's a conversation you keep putting off. *Now* is your moment to step in and finish what you've started! Write down that one area and commit to confront and approach it today. You're a revolutionary, and nothing can hinder your ability to live, love and lead from your heart!

_____

_____

_____

_____

_____

For some of you, finishing this journey has been the longest you've ever stayed committed to anything. But you did it! You let God capture your heart and revolutionize your life. Know today with confidence that you are the true essence and reflection of the Heart Revolution. You are not the same. You have taken a stand to overthrow mindsets, customs, and traditions that you once carried in your heart. And, more importantly, you've established a new precedent in your life, a precedent that begins and ends at the core of your being—your heart. You have turned your heart back to God and back to your family and developed your God-given potential. Now it's time to begin to advance His kingdom, first throughout your circles of influence, and then, as He gives you opportunity, to the nations abroad.

In all that you do, stay true to your heart and stay strong in your faith. Don't let the joy of knowing, loving, and serving Jesus escape from the corridors of your heart. Remember, no one is expecting perfection out of you—only progress. Take time in God's presence daily to replenish your heart with His truth and love. And when you need a reminder of all that He has done in your life, flip through these pages again and revive the revolution on the inside of you. You are His son, His daughter, and His answer to the world. You are His revolutionary who has been chosen, set apart, and anointed to turn hearts back to Him. His heart now beats in unison with yours and nothing is out of your reach. This Heart Revolution is alive in every word you speak, every action you take, and in every heart decision you make.

That's because this revolution will always be about one thing—your heart.

Notes

1. J. I. Packer, *Knowing God* (Downers Grove, IL: InterVarsity, 1973), 227.

2. Philip Yancey, *Reaching for the Invisible God* (Grand Rapids: Zondervan, 2000), 69.

3. Marianne Williamson, *A Return to Love: Reflections on the Principles of a Course in Miracles* (New York: HarperPerennial, 1996), 190–91.

4. Paul Tournier, *The Meaning of Persons* (Cutchogue, NY: Buccaneer, 1999).

5. Packer, *Knowing God*, 74.

6. Josh McDowell, *One Year Book of Youth Devotions*, vol. 2 (Wheaton: Tyndale, 2003), 275.

Special Thanks

First and foremost, to my Lord and Savior Jesus Christ, who turned my heart and gave me a mission and vision to live for!

To my gorgeous, anointed, and amazing wife, Georgina, who has held my ladder since the day I married her! I am in constant awe of the phenomenal wife, mother, pastor, and worship leader that you are. Without your yes, Cornerstone Church of San Diego would not be what it is today. I love you, Georgi!

To my six beautiful daughters—Selena, Crystal, Carissa, Alexis, Angel, and Miracle—you each have all far surpassed my own aspirations for you! I am proud of who each of you is becoming as you allow the hand of God to form you for His purposes. Being your father has made me a better husband, a better man, and a better pastor. I love you girls with all my heart and thank God that I have the privilege to be your dad!

To the entire De La Mora family, for your unconditional love, unending support, and unwavering faith in me. I am grateful for being able to say I come from one the greatest families in the world!

To my pastors, Art and Kuna Sepúlveda, who have believed in me, discipled me, and poured their hearts into me. I honor you for your wisdom, leadership, and inspiration that have set a standard in my life and ministry that I strive to attain every day. I am honored to have both of you as my spiritual parents!

To the entire Cornerstone Church family, for dreaming, believing, praying, fasting, inviting, and giving to see people experience the power of a turned heart. *We did it!* Because of you, the heart behind this revolution will continue to flow from God's heart to the nation!

To my amazing Staff, Assistant Pastors, and Team 12 leaders, who have consistently run wholeheartedly with every vision God entrusted to me year after year and never said no. I couldn't do what God is asking me to do without you! You have personified the core value: *"When the team works, the dream works!"* Come on, somebody!

To Derick and Leticia Ventura, the covenant couple whose creative genius has embodied the heart and vision of my ministry. You both have brought to life, in artistic and literary form, the mission of this church and the passion of my heart! Your legacy will forever be in print for David, Annabella, and Ava!

To Duncan Dodds, for always reminding me to stay true to the brand, go big with the brand, and become the brand! Your friendship, honest feedback, and loyalty has made this dream come alive. You are a true revolutionary!

To the entire staff at Baker Books, for taking the risk and launching out into the deep with me. Your work ethic and spirit of excellence have made this book a reality!

Sergio De La Mora is the visionary founder and pastor of Cornerstone Church of San Diego, California, one of the fastest growing churches in America. Called "The Turn-Around Specialist," Sergio De La Mora has influenced a multigenerational and multicultural community in both English and Spanish for more than a decade. Under Sergio's leadership, Cornerstone Church has a weekly congregation of over 5,000, evolving from the ground up. Cornerstone Church has steadily continued to grow in size and impact—a testament to Sergio's understanding, skill, commitment, and unique approach to advancing the kingdom for Christ throughout the community.

As a leading voice in the Latino community, he has been featured several times on TBN, the world's largest religious television network. A board member for Joel Osteen's Champion Network, Sergio serves as one of the Partnering Pastors for Night of Hope in New York, Los Angeles, and Jerusalem. In 2008 Sergio De La Mora launched the Heart Revolution Conference, gathering well-known thought leaders from all over the nation with the purpose of revolutionizing the hearts of the next generation.

His weekly television and radio broadcasts, *The Power of a Turned Heart*, empower thousands to live, love, and lead from their heart. He is cofounder of the Turning the Hearts Center, a nonprofit organization designed to empower youth and families and restore family unity and self-sufficiency through a variety of programs, seminars, and support resources.

Sergio De La Mora lives in San Diego, California, with his wife, Georgina, and their six daughters.

Watch video messages from Pastor Sergio and find information on the 40-Day Heart Challenge

www.sergiodelamora.com/heartrev

and Connect at

 Sergio De La Mora

 PastorSergio  PastorGeorgina

 theheartrev

BakerBooks
a division of Baker Publishing Group
www.BakerBooks.com